3 1994 01454 6813

2/12

how to start a home-based

Bookkeeping Business

Michelle Long

gPP®

Guilford, Connecticut

657.2068 LON
Long, Michelle L.
How to start a home-based
bookkeeping business

$18.95
CENTRAL   31994014546813

To buy books in quantity for corporate use
or incentives, call **(800) 962-0973**
or e-mail **premiums@GlobePequot.com**.

Copyright © 2011 by Morris Book Publishing, LLC

ALL RIGHTS RESERVED. No part of this book may be reproduced or transmitted in any form by any means, electronic or mechanical, including photocopying and recording, or by any information storage and retrieval system, except as may be expressly permitted in writing from the publisher. Requests for permission should be addressed to Globe Pequot Press, Attn: Rights and Permissions Department, P.O. Box 480, Guilford, CT 06437.

Editorial Director: Cynthia Hughes
Editor: Katie Benoit
Project Editor: Tracee Williams
Text Design: Sheryl P. Kober
Layout: Kevin Mak

Chart on pages 62–63 is provided by the law office of Richard E. Gier, PA, www.GierLaw.com.
Graph on page 131 is courtesy of HubSpot, State of Inbound Marketing Report, http://bit.ly/aewfHr.
Text on pages 141–44 courtesy of Intuit Inc. © 2005 Intuit Inc. All rights reserved. Intuit, the Intuit logo, and QuickBooks, among others, are registered trademarks and/or registered service marks of Intuit Inc. in the United States and other countries. Other parties' trademarks or service marks are the property of their respective owners and should be treated as such.
Text on pages 156–61 courtesy of Intuit Inc.
Text on pages 164–68 is reprinted in its entirety with permission from Intuit Inc.
Text for appendix B courtesy of Jay Shah
Diagrams for appendix B courtesy of Dr. Chandra Bhansali

Library of Congress Cataloging-in-Publication Data is available on file.

ISBN 978-0-7627-6126-5

Printed in the United States of America
10 9 8 7 6 5 4 3 2 1

This book's purpose is to provide accurate and authoritative information on the topics covered. It is sold with the understanding that neither the author nor the publisher is engaged in rendering legal, financial, accounting, and other professional services. Neither Globe Pequot Press nor the author assumes any liability resulting from action taken based on the information included herein. Mention of a company name does not constitute endorsement.

This book is dedicated to all the bookkeepers and accountants in pursuit of their own home-based business. Starting my own home-based accounting practice in 1991 was one of the best decisions I have ever made. I hope this book helps you build your own successful home-based bookkeeping business, too.

Contents

Acknowledgments

I have many people to thank and acknowledge for their help in writing this book.

First and foremost is my family. Special thanks to my husband, Steve, and my children, Andrew and Jessica, for your support and encouragement while I was writing this book—especially when deadlines were approaching and I questioned whether I could get it done. You helped me stay focused and determined to finish it, and I am so grateful for your support. I appreciate the help and understanding from you all!

Many people helped me write this book without even realizing it. Thank you to the bookkeepers, accountants, QuickBooks ProAdvisors, tax professionals, IT consultants, and others who participated online in my LinkedIn Group (Successful QuickBooks Consultants), Intuit Community Forums, the American Institute of Professional Bookkeepers (AIPB) discussion list, and other online groups and forums. Reading their questions and the advice and experience they share with each other helped me focus on the most important and relevant topics and concepts for this book. I would like to especially thank those who provided quotes that are included throughout the book and Jay Shah for writing an article about the accounting industry and cloud computing (included in the appendices).

Thank you, Intuit, for permission to include the Average Billing Rates Survey, sample engagement letters, and QuickBooks New Client Setup Checklist in this book. Those resources and others provided to accounting professionals via Intuit Academy and the QuickBooks ProAdvisor Program have helped me achieve success in my business. Additionally, I am honored and grateful to be a member of Intuit's Writer/Trainer Network and one of the few national trainers for Intuit's "What's New" launch tour each autumn. I truly enjoy helping other accounting professionals learn more about QuickBooks and helping them grow their business.

To everyone at Globe Pequot Press: Thank you for allowing me to be an author for your home-based business series of books. I am thrilled to be fortunate enough to have the opportunity to write a book for your series. I appreciate your assistance and efforts to the book.

To the new home-based bookkeepers and accountants: Congratulations on starting your own business! I am sure this book will help you on the road to building your own successful business. Being a home-based business owner is not always easy, but I think it is definitely worth the effort. It takes some time and patience, but you can do it, and this book will help you.

Lastly I'd like to thank all the clients who allow me into their worlds to share, learn, grow, and experience this passion of mine. I truly enjoy every minute with you and am grateful that you open your world and trust me to support you on this journey.

Introduction

Many years ago Benjamin Franklin said, "There is nothing certain in life except death and taxes." This is still true today. The certainty of taxes, combined with the confusing and complex tax laws, creates a continuous demand for bookkeeping, accounting services, and tax preparation. In 2009 the United States had about 27.5 million small businesses, according to the Small Business Administration's Office of Advocacy, and about 552,600 new businesses in 2009.

According to the laws of the Internal Revenue Service, businesses "must keep adequate accounting records." The vast majority of small businesses need help to comply with that law. This fact creates an ongoing, continuous demand for accounting services.

I realized this fact when I was in college and needed to choose my major. I could not decide whether to major in accounting or finance. As I debated which major I should choose, I thought about what type of job I might have in the future. I considered that I might need to get a job in various cities (depending on where my future husband was working), so I wanted something that would be needed wherever I might live. I decided that with an accounting degree, I could get a job anywhere because most businesses need accountants. Plus, every city has accounting firms. And, if I became a certified public accountant, then someday I could start my own practice.

The accounting industry provides many options and opportunities, and the demand for accounting services is always there, no matter what the economic conditions or where you live accounting services have several areas, so you can specialize in an area that interests you.

When I started my home-based accounting business (in 1991), I provided the traditional accounting services—monthly bookkeeping, payroll, and tax preparation. Over the years I have changed the services I provide to focus on what I enjoy (one of the benefits of being your own boss). Now I provide QuickBooks consulting and training, and I work with small business owners (including accounting professionals), coaching and helping them grow their business. I am one of the national trainers and writers for Intuit, and I teach other accounting professionals about QuickBooks. I have been a consultant for product development for Intuit, where I was able to work with the programmers on new features and enhancements. Best of all, I am doing what I truly enjoy.

Whether you are a bookkeeper or an accountant (these terms, along with *accounting professionals*, will be used interchangeably throughout this book), this industry has so many opportunities. Many small businesses will continue to need someone to do the monthly bookkeeping for them. Or, if they decide to do it on their own, they will need training, support, and clean-up work as well. Plus, if clients do not need your assistance with daily transactions, then you may be able to provide them with other consulting services.

Changing technology, such as the Internet, remote access, and social media, has created even more opportunities for accounting professionals. Increasing numbers of bookkeepers operate virtually with clients nationwide, and they do everything online. Clients are becoming more comfortable with doing business online (online banking, online bill pay, Facebook, and more), and they are more willing to incorporate online services into their businesses.

With the information in this book, you will be able to start your own home-based bookkeeping business and begin pursuing the opportunities that are available. This book will help you consider whether being self-employed and running a home-based business are right for you. We will cover the initial steps to starting your business from choosing a name to selecting the type of entity and more. We will discuss the importance and components of a business plan. Chapters on marketing include details about creating a website and how to utilize social media. There is a chapter on financial considerations as well as a chapter on client-management, legal, and ethical issues. You will find checklists and other resources to help you get your home-based bookkeeping business started on the road to success.

So You Want to Start a Bookkeeping Business

Many people dream about starting their own business and being their own boss. They envision how wonderful it will be to have a flexible schedule and all the other benefits of self-employment. However, the reality of being self-employed is not as wonderful as people usually envision. The reality is that being self-employed is a lot of hard work. You will spend a lot of time and energy getting the business started and then managing and growing the business. Self-employed people often realize that they work much harder than they did when they were employees but find the work more fulfilling because it is their own business.

Before you quit your job to pursue your entrepreneurial dream, it is important to consider whether self-employment is for you. This chapter will help you do some self-assessment and introspection to see if you are really suited for self-employment and help you realize the benefits of being an employee as well as the pros and cons of self-employment.

How the Industry Has Changed

The bookkeeping industry has changed quite a bit over the years, and those green columnar pads are a thing of the past. Significant changes in technology have occurred, and increasingly complex rules and regulations affect the industry for accounting services.

Technology has enabled some small businesses to use QuickBooks or another accounting application to do some of their own bookkeeping. However, these small business owners generally need help with setup and training to learn how to properly enter transactions. After the initial setup, they often need assistance on a monthly or quarterly basis as well. They may need assistance making reconciliations, recording the purchase of a vehicle, figuring payroll, performing year-end tasks, or cleaning up mistakes they made when entering things incorrectly.

Improvements in technology have enabled us to work remotely with clients from anywhere so geographic boundaries are no longer important. You can have clients from coast to coast or work remotely when you are traveling. With our ability to scan and e-mail documents, access client computers remotely, and even use webcams, virtual offices and remote bookkeeping are becoming more common.

In the appendices is an interesting article written by Jay Shah that examines the changes and evolution of the accounting industry. It helps explain the changes in technology and how the changes have affected accounting services.

In addition, continuous changes have occurred in the rules and regulations for income, sales and payroll taxes, and other government or industry compliance issues. These continuous changes make it challenging to stay current with the latest rules, requirements, and regulations. It is challenging to "know it all" regardless of whether you work as a home-based sole practitioner or work in an accounting office with others. As a result many bookkeepers choose to specialize in a certain industry or to provide only certain services. For example, I no longer provide payroll or tax services; I decided it was too difficult to keep abreast of the ever-changing rules and regulations. I am aware of the general rules and regulations, but I do not try to keep abreast of all the details and intricacies. Instead, I refer clients to other accounting professionals for services such as tax preparation or payroll services. Doing this has allowed me to specialize in an area that I enjoy—QuickBooks consulting and training.

Why? Your Motivation for Starting Your Own Business

When my first child was born, I took a six-month maternity leave from work. After a couple of months I realized that I did not want to go back to a full-time job outside the home. That is when I decided I wanted to start my own home-based accounting practice. My initial motivation was to stay home with my son and earn enough money to help cover our monthly expenses. (I was fortunate that my husband had a good job with health insurance, which made it easier financially.) My business has evolved over the years as far as the services I provide, but I have always been home-based.

People start their own business for a variety of reasons. What is your motivation for starting your own business? Perhaps you lost your job as a result of a struggling economy and have been unable to get another job. Maybe you have always wanted to start your own business and took a buyout from your employer to quit, or you just quit. Maybe you are still working but are eager to go out on your own. Your motivation for starting your own business may affect your vision and plans for the business.

Regardless of why you want to start your own business, what are important are your desire and passion for it. It is hard work to start your own business, and doing so takes time and energy. Your strong desire and passion will help you be successful and persevere through the long hours and challenges you will face. Your drive to succeed may be financial, especially if you need the income to support yourself or your family. Maybe you truly love bookkeeping or taxes and are excited to be doing what you love. Or perhaps you have a strong desire to be self-employed and have the skills and experience for a bookkeeping business. Whatever your reason, having a strong desire and passion will help you be successful.

Is Self-Employment for You?

It is common to hear people talk about how much they would like to quit their job and be their own boss. They could get away from their terrible boss and annoying co-workers. They are sick and tired of working long hours when no one seems to appreciate their work. They dream about being self-employed, being an entrepreneur, and starting their own business. They believe self-employment will provide them with so much freedom and flexibility. They dream of the wonderful joys that self-employment would bring. Unfortunately it is a dream. The reality is that although being self-employed has many benefits, it is not easy. Being self-employed is not for everyone.

Most people have been an employee at some point in their life, perhaps in many positions or companies. For many it's easy to know what it is like to be an employee, but they may not know what it is really like to be self-employed. How are self-employed working conditions different than those of an employee? Look at the chart on page 4 and compare the characteristics.

As you can see, you have many uncertainties when you are self-employed. After your business is established, you usually work more hours than you did when you were an employee. When you are self-employed, you have to do all administrative tasks, marketing, and many other tasks that you did not have to worry about as an employee. As you look at the differences between employees and self-employed workers, consider which one is right for you.

	Employee	Self-employed
Work Hours	Specified hours (8–5)	Vary greatly—you have to work as much as required to get the work done.
Paycheck	Every payday	Uncertain and varies—plus, you have to invoice and collect payment, too!
Breaks/Lunch Hour	Defined times	Sometimes there is no time for a break or lunch.
Overtime Pay	If hourly or maybe comp time off	Same billing rate
Sick/Vacation Days	May be paid	Unpaid and maybe no time for it
Holidays	May be paid	Unpaid and maybe no time for it
Health Insurance	May be employer provided or discounted	Expensive
Stress and Worry	Usually none when you go home	Always—the buck stops with you!
Office Furniture, Computer, Software, Copier, and Supplies	Provided	Up to you
Admin, IT, HR, or Other Help	Available	You're on your own—make copies, purchase office supplies, empty trash, update computers, answer phones, market your business, and more. You do it all!
Ultimate Responsibility to Clients	Your bosses	You're it—if you make a mistake, or a client is unhappy, it is your responsibility.
Resources and Support	Usually there are other people for questions, training, or support.	You're it!
Training and Continuing Education	May be provided or paid for	Up to you

On the other hand, being self-employed has many benefits. A few key benefits of self-employment include:

1. Flexible hours and work schedule

I'm not a morning person, and I would rather stay up late working. I know some morning people who enjoy getting up early and working several hours before breakfast. As long as the work gets done, it doesn't matter when you work. You can work when you are most productive. Instead of struggling to stay awake in the afternoon, you can do something else during that time.

You can take some time off during the week or whenever needed. The freedom and flexible schedule are two of the main benefits of self-employment. This is why I quit the corporate world and went out on my own. As a new mom, I wanted to be able to attend school events, go on field trips, or do other family-oriented things with my kids. Whether you need to renew a driver's license, go to the dentist or doctor, or help with sick or aging parents, having a flexible schedule can be a tremendous benefit. After all, sometimes you may just want to take an afternoon off to enjoy the spring weather!

2. Select the services you provide and the clients you want

Instead of having a boss telling what you have to do, you can choose what type of work or services you want to provide. After I graduated from college, I went to work for a public accounting firm. During tax season we had to work on taxes in addition to the audit work. I never liked taxes—not even the tax classes I had in college! For several months I had to do work that I neither liked nor enjoyed for seventy to eighty hours a week (or more). Now that I am self-employed, I do not offer tax services anymore.

In addition, when you are self-employed, you can select the clients and industries that interest you. Many accounting firms assign staff members to work on clients without input from those members as to their preferences. For example, if you are assigned to work on a client in the health care industry, then you are likely to be scheduled to work on another health care client because you have experience in that industry. Before you know it, you are pigeon-holed in a certain industry, whether you like it or not. When you are self-employed, you can choose the clients or industries that you'd like to work for based on your interests and preferences.

What Is the Best Thing about Working from Home?

For me, it's not having to worry about snowstorms or traffic when commuting to work. I did that for close to twenty-five years, and I don't miss it at all. I love being able to set my own hours. I work only part-time these days, so I have the flexibility of scheduling my on-site clients at my convenience. The rest of my clients' work gets done at odd hours of my own choosing.

Laura Lincoln, Sound Bookkeeping Services,
www.soundbookkeeping.com, South Yarmouth, MA

I think the best thing about working from home is the flexibility that it allows. We remote in to a lot of our clients, so we have a tendency to work later in the evening. We use the other time to allow us to do what we need to do: some networking luncheons, business meetings, etc. I also like the fact it cuts my overhead costs by not needing to pay rent for an office, phone, Internet—all the things that go into having an office outside of the home.

Martin G. Meyer, B. Meyer Bookkeeping Solutions,
www.bmeyerbookkeeping.com, Sugar Land, TX

3. Select with whom you want to work

As an employee, you may not like your boss or co-workers. Perhaps your boss is almost intolerable, or you have a co-worker who is so annoying that you hate going to work every day. Maybe you are assigned to work with clients who are disrespectful or otherwise not enjoyable. As an employee, you may not be able to do much to change the situation.

When you are self-employed, you can choose the clients you work with. If you do not like someone for whatever reason, then you do not have to work with that person. If a client is always late, does not provide the information needed, wants to take questionable deductions, treats you with disrespect, or for whatever reason, then you can fire that client.

4. Have unlimited income potential

As an employee, you are paid a specified amount—either hourly or a salary. You may be eligible for a bonus, but your income is essentially set and limited. If you are an employee of an accounting firm, and you bring in new clients, your compensation does not increase as a result of your efforts (in most cases).

On the other hand, when you are self-employed, your income potential is unlimited. The amount you earn is a direct result of your efforts, skills, and abilities. So, if you work many hours and get new clients, you reap the rewards of your efforts.

5. Avoid rush hour

If you are self-employed, you can schedule your appointments or meetings to avoid rush hour. If you have driven in rush hour traffic for any length of time, then you will really appreciate this benefit. I never schedule things before 9:00 a.m. so that I miss the morning rush hour. In the afternoons I usually try to finish up so that I can get home before the evening rush.

6. Create your own work environment

Instead of commuting to work every day, you can save time and instead work from your home office. You do not have to worry about wearing business casual attire. Unless you are meeting with clients, you can work in your PJs and slippers. You can work in your home office, on the back deck, at the lake, on a beach, or wherever is most beneficial for you.

Personal Characteristics or Traits

Certain personal characteristics, traits, skills, and abilities are needed to be a small business owner or successful entrepreneur. Some of these tend to be natural personality characteristics, whereas others may be skills or abilities that can be nurtured or developed over time. Either way, it is important to do an honest assessment of yourself so you know your areas of strength and where you need to improve.

Use the chart on pages 8-9 to perform an objective self-assessment to see if you have the personal characteristics you will need to start and run your own bookkeeping business. Do not expect to be strong in all areas. Instead, use this chart to help you understand and be more aware of your strengths and weaknesses.

Why Be a Home-Based Business?

Today over half of all U.S. businesses are home-based. But in the past being a home-based business was not as widely accepted as it is today. People would try to hide the fact that they ran a home-based business. In an effort to appear that they were

Assessment of Personal Characteristics

	Strength	Adequate	Needs Improvement
Self-discipline—you have no boss asking how you are doing or checking on your work. You need self-discipline to get the work done.			
Reliability and dependability—clients can depend on you to be available and you can be relied upon to act quickly and efficiently.			
Utmost integrity and ethical behavior—you are dealing with sensitive financial information, and client confidentiality is essential. It is important to comply with all rules and regulations, and your clients should as well.			
Good communication and interpersonal skills (written and oral)—you need to be able to communicate effectively with clients, potential clients, vendors, banks, or others.			
Resourcefulness—you need to be able to seek out help, information, or whatever you need and be diligent in obtaining this information.			
Persistence and patience—it takes time to get clients and build the business. Don't expect to be successful overnight. You need to consistently market and network with others.			

	Strength	Adequate	Needs Improvement
Organization and time management—you must meet due dates or deadlines, maintain client records, track your time for billing purposes, and operate efficiently.			
Continuous learning—you need to stay current with rules and regulations in the industry, changing software, and technology.			
Ability to deal with uncertainty—you need to be prepared to sometimes unearth more questions than answers, and have sudden and unexpected situations arise.			
Determination and resiliency—problems or mistakes will occur. You will lose some clients, computers or equipment will break or fail, and other things will go wrong. You have to be able to deal with it and move on.			
Self-confidence—if you do not have confidence in yourself, then clients will not either. You do not have to know it all, but you need to be able to learn more or find the answer/help needed.			
Networking—you do not have to be a social butterfly, but you do need to constantly network with others, both in person and online, to help grow your business and brand.			

located in an office building, some people would use "Suite B" (basement) or "Suite A" (attic) as part of their address. Thanks to the growing popularity of home-based businesses today, this mind-set has changed among business owners.

A service-based business such as bookkeeping is especially suited to being a home-based business. Usually clients do not need to actually come to your office. In the event that you do need to meet with a client, you can have a quick meeting in a coffee shop or other public places. With the technology available, you can work with clients from coast to coast, Hawaii, Alaska, or other countries. You are not limited to a geographic area anymore.

Some people think they need an office to be a legitimate business. Ask yourself why you think you need or want an office. Why incur the overhead costs of an office when it does not matter to your clients or potential clients? The additional costs of renting an office (rent, utilities, phone, Internet access, and more) are a burden that can be avoided. When you start your business, you can minimize the risks and costs involved by making your office home-based.

Balancing Work and Family

Your family needs will change depending on whether you deal with young children, aging parents, illnesses, or any number of other situations that may arise. That is one of the best aspects of being self-employed—the flexibility you have in your schedule. As long as the work gets done, you can do it when it is convenient for you. However, if you do not set boundaries, it is easy for work to take too much time or attention away from your family (and vice versa). You should try to keep a balance between the two and adapt to meet the needs of your family and job.

Think about when you want to work. Do you want to be available nights and weekends for your family? Do you want to work while you are on vacation, or is this time off limits? Or will it depend on the needs of your clients? For example, I had a client who wanted me to be "on-call" when I was on vacation. So, we discussed the ground rules for our communication during this time (i.e., the client could call only so many times a day) and a reasonable fee for my "on-call" services. The client was happy, and I was willing to do it, too. You get to set your own rules. You should inform your clients about your rules and then enforce them. Do not let clients take advantage of you and your time.

Both Sides of the Ledger

What is the best thing about working from home? I get up, grab a cup of coffee, and check my e-mails, forums, etc. I make my phone calls first thing, and when I have contacted everyone I need to get info from (get them working), then I go work out or ride my horse, shower, and go to work for the rest of the day. My clients don't know that I take a good part of the morning off. I like the flexibility. I often work until late in the evening. I love that I don't have to listen to unhappy co-workers complain about the boss or husband or client or mailman, etc. I am fairly sensitive to noise, so my home office works great. (I live alone, so only the dogs get in trouble for being noisy.)

What do you not like about working from home? When I meet clients at my home office, I feel the need to clean the whole house, not just the office. It aggravates me when clients don't show up. I do get nervous about meeting clients at my home. Neighbors and friends think that, since my schedule is flexible, I can talk or go out any time, I get a lot of drop-ins, and sometimes feelings get hurt when I tell them that they need to leave because I am working. Some people think that because I don't go to an off-site office for my job I don't actually work.

Do you have any advice or suggestions for others wanting to start working from home? After working from home for the last four years or so, I decided to get an off-site office in order to get out of the house more often. I found one in a great building that was dirt cheap, had a beautiful view and nice people, and was pet-friendly. The only downside is that it is a half-hour away. I do like the office but still find myself working from home more than at the office. I will probably not renew when my lease is up and instead spend the money on a housekeeper rather than rent. None of my clients cares at all whether I work from home or from an office. But my clients do love that I always return their calls/e-mails within twenty-four hours, no matter where I am.

Lori Thompson, KTJ Tax, www.KTJtax.com, Paw Paw, IL

Adapting Your Business to Meet Changing Family Needs

I started my home-based accounting business when my first child was born so I could be home with him. When my kids were little, I used Mother's Day Out for a few days a week so I could get some work done. After my kids were in school, I had more time for work, but I did not work nights or weekends. I was very involved with PTA and school events, and I kept the business at a manageable level. I learned to fire some clients, and I quit doing taxes (which I never liked to do). Soon my kids were in middle school and high school, and I had more time to grow the business. I started doing what I really enjoy—teaching and training, which did involve some nights, weekends, and travel.

Now, when we go on vacation or to the lake, I sometimes work remotely with clients. For example, I have helped clients from the ski lodge in the mountains of Colorado (I need a break from skiing anyway). Or, on vacation in Florida, I took a break from the beach, went to the room, and had a one-hour training session with a client. With technology I can work from anywhere or anytime that I choose to schedule an appointment.

Do You Have the Skills and Experience?

When I started my own accounting business, I thought it would be relatively easy. After all, I had a degree in accounting, and I am a CPA. I had worked in public accounting for three years auditing companies from various industries and doing some tax returns. Plus, I had worked at a large private company for three years where one of my positions had been in corporate financial reporting and consolidation. Surely I could do the bookkeeping and taxes for small businesses, right? I quickly realized that I still needed to learn a lot. For example, I knew how to accrue payroll for the year-end journal entries. However, I did not know how to process payroll or all the various due dates and filing requirements. Same thing for sales taxes—I needed to learn about those, too. I quickly realized how much I did not know, and I had to learn as I went along. I had to find resources and seminars to help me.

You need to assess your bookkeeping skills and experience to determine if you are ready to go out on your own. You may need to take some classes or learn more to be better prepared. A degree in accounting is not required, but you need to make sure you know the basics of accounting or bookkeeping. Your local community college usually offers accounting classes with affordable tuition (typically $75–$150 per credit hour). Often the community college allow an individual to take some classes

Home, Sweet Home

How is your home office set up? I use a spare bedroom. My office started out to be two tables and a chair. Twenty years later, I have three desks, fax machine and copier stands, two computers, three printers, a bookshelf and a filing cabinet. I can barely turn around!

What is the best thing about working from home? Setting my own schedule. Don't have to worry about the weather or traffic unless I have to go out for an appointment. Nobody knows that I'm having a bad hair day!

What do you not like about working from home? The solitude and not having that personal interaction with other professional people. The various online community forums help with that, but nothing can replace live, in your face, human contact. Also, my family didn't always respect the fact that I was "at work" when I was home.

Do you have any advice or suggestions for others wanting to start working from home?
It takes a very disciplined individual to work alone at home. Working at home requires a lot of self-control and self-motivation. There's nobody there to make sure you clock in and get your job done. There are a lot of distractions when you're in your home all day; laundry needs to be done; you see the dust on the furniture as you get your third cup of coffee; dinner may need to be started; personal telephone calls come in; friends and neighbors who know you are home may visit, etc. There's always the temptation to do something else and work later.

Cindy Plumley, Hallmark Bookkeeping, Chesterfield, VA

as a non-degree seeking student. At a minimum, you may want to take a couple of accounting courses to learn the basics.

It would be helpful to have accounting or bookkeeping experience before you start your own business. The challenge is to discover where to get this experience. Check with the job placement department of your local community college. Many times small businesses have listings for a student for basic bookkeeping tasks. This can be a great way to start getting experience. Other places to look for a bookkeeping job include Craigslist, local classifieds, and LinkedIn. Some small nonprofit organizations may need your help as well. Consider churches, homeowners' associations, PTAs, scouts, or others who might appreciate your assistance. If you work for a small nonprofit organization, your work may be unpaid but will help you get experience.

Another way to get experience is to work for another accountant/bookkeeper. Contact sole proprietors or small firms. They usually hire help before busy season starts, so it's best to contact them in the autumn. If they do not need a full-time person, see if they could use you on a part-time basis as a subcontractor. Remember that you are trying to learn more and get on-the-job training so you can reach your goal of starting your own business.

If you already have the education and experience, then you may find that you need to learn more about special topics or areas. Numerous seminars and webinars are available on a variety of topics. You might be amazed by how many free webinars are available online on a variety of topics. Use search engines such as Google or online viewing sites such as YouTube to find ones on the topic you need. Or check with local organizations (a Small Business Development Center, Service Corps of Retired Executives [SCORE], and others) for seminars.

Do not feel that you have to know it all before you get started—you will never know it all! Things that will be new to you will always come up in this business You need to know the basics and how to research to find the answers or where you can get help when needed. This is how you learn from experience. Over time you will learn when to turn down a client or project that exceeds your abilities, especially if you know your capabilities and limitations. For example, you may know how to do corporate tax returns. However, you may not be ready to do taxes for a multinational corporation with a number of subsidiaries or other complex tax situations.

Financial Considerations

Finally, before you start your own business, it is a good idea to consider your personal financial situation. Remember that it takes time to build a business and a solid client base. It will take time to get the first few clients—you need to be prepared financially during this time. When planning for your business, you need to factor in start-up costs. For a home-based bookkeeping business, the start-up costs are not significant compared with those of some businesses.

Prior to starting your business, it is a good idea to have money saved to cover several months of living expenses (perhaps six to twelve months) to ensure you can support the business during the time it takes to build it up. If you have a family, it is important to discuss your plans with your spouse or significant other prior to starting your business. You want his or her support in starting your business. Communication is important in alleviating tension and misunderstandings.

If you are currently employed, you might consider starting your business part-time. Perhaps you want to work on your business nights and weekends initially. Doing this allows you to get your first few clients and establish a base before you quit your job. Although you will be working a lot, and it will be tiring, it is less risky and can help with the financial transition from employee to self-employed.

Working Smarter, Not Harder

What is the best thing about working from home? The freedom of working whenever! But that took some time as I slowly converted my clients so that I could work remotely. Working remotely really is the key but I am not totally there yet on working remotely and paperless. I start working early way before my clients even get in their offices. I check banking (all a keystroke preset on my keyboard), read, and send e-mails for the morning. I work a few hours on tasks such as online bill paying, invoicing, and inputting Accounts Payable invoices from scans from my e-mails. Then I go play tennis if it's a nice day or go for a run. I just love that I have these options. I only wish I had streamlined myself much sooner with the remote bookkeeping and online availabilities (online banking!). I just told someone yesterday that I feel semiretired, but in actuality I am busier than I have ever been. Like the old saying, it's about working smarter, not harder!

What do you not like about working from home? I am not as organized as I would like to be. I find that I will start working (log in) on one client, log in to another client account, and go from one client to another. I go back and forth without sometimes finishing. If I was in my client's office, I would take care of the tasks for that client only, finish, and then move on the next client.

Joan Miceli-Muhlbauer, Computer Ledger Systems,
www.computerledgersystems.com, Hopewell Junction, NY

Think about your ultimate goal and vision for your business. It is helpful to have a clear picture of what you envision for your business in the future. What do you want the business to be like in five years, ten years, or more? Stephen Covey, author of *7 Habits of Highly Effective People*, says, "Begin with the end in mind."

What Is Your Vision for the Business?

Everyone starts a business with the idea that it will be successful. But what does that mean? What is a successful business? Is success based on gross revenue? The number of clients or employees? The number of locations? What constitutes a successful business? Whether your business is a success or not depends on your definition of success and your personal goals for your business.

Close your eyes for a few minutes and visualize your business five years from now. Envision the ideal business for you if there were no limitations on time or money. What would your business look like? Think about the following in regard to how each relates to your ideal business:

- Are you a sole proprietor, or do you have employees or subcontractors?
- What is your office like? Are you home-based? Do you have a physical office location? Do you work with employees or subcontractors via a virtual office (i.e., utilizing online technologies)? Do you have multiple office locations?
- What do you do all day? Are you managing employees, reviewing their work and training them? Are you out networking and marketing the

Successful Businesses May Look Different

Betty's Bookkeeping Services: Betty started her home-based bookkeeping business ten years ago. She provides monthly bookkeeping services, processes payroll, and does QuickBooks consulting. Betty refers her clients to a couple of CPAs to prepare their income tax returns at year's end. In return the CPAs often refer bookkeeping or QuickBooks services to her. Betty loves what she does and enjoys cleaning up a good bookkeeping mess. She works lots of hours, but her net income is over $100,000 a year (after putting money into a retirement fund). Betty also takes five or six weeks of vacation a year. When she is on vacation, she can work remotely if necessary, but she usually schedules vacations around various due dates.

Tom's Tax and Accounting: Tom opened his first office ten years ago and now has three offices. Each office has an office manager and three to five employees. They provide monthly bookkeeping, payroll services, and tax return preparation. In the autumn they have training for the upcoming tax season when each office will prepare hundreds of returns. Tom rotates between the offices reviewing the work and dealing with the difficult returns or accounting issues. After busy season Tom takes a week of vacation and usually squeezes in another week during the year. Tom has a retirement plan and receives over $100,000 per year for his salary.

Both Tom and Betty are happy and consider their businesses successful. Betty likes the freedom and flexibility of operating alone so she can decide how much to work. She likes to take time off for family and friends and does not want to worry about employees. Tom enjoys managing employees and having multiple offices. He is planning to sell the business soon to spend more time with family and friends. They both created a successful business for their individual situation, but each business is vastly different.

business? What type of work are you doing (taxes, bookkeeping, payroll, consulting, etc.)? How many hours do you work?

- What types of clients are you working with? How big are their businesses? What types of industries? How many clients?

- Financially, what is your annual income from the business? Do you have a retirement plan set up?

Keep this vision of your ideal business in mind as you plan and start your business. Focusing on your ultimate goal can help guide you as you plan and build your business.

What Services to Offer?

When you are starting your own bookkeeping business, one of the first things you need to decide is what services to provide. If you are like most people, you will decide to offer all types of accounting and bookkeeping services and anything else that clients might need and will pay you to do for them. After all, you are just starting, and you do not have any work or clients yet. Let's consider this approach from the client's perspective. Here is a sample list of services that might be listed on a website:

- QuickBooks training
- QuickBooks setup and clean-up
- Bookkeeping services for small business and individuals
- Payroll
- Accounts receivable
- Personal day-to-day monthly billings
- Bank reconciliation
- Accounts payable
- General ledger preparation
- Cash flow management
- Word processing
- Financial statement preparation
- Virtual assistance
- Internet research

Pretend that you are a small business needing monthly bookkeeping or payroll services. As you look at this list of services, you have the following observations:

- The company provides services for individuals and businesses, word processing, virtual assistance, and Internet research—perhaps with such a variety of services, this person is desperate for work.

- The company lists out accounts receivable, accounts payable, general ledger preparation—why not just say "monthly bookkeeping services"? (I have seen some websites that list out every task or report. Are the companies trying to make it look like they do more?)
- Notice the confusing service of "personal day-to-day monthly billings"—is it day-to-day or monthly, and what does that mean? Perhaps it means the company handles the monthly bills received (like utilities and others) on a daily basis?
- Is the "cash flow management" for my business or personal?

To a potential client, the company may not seem to be focused. This appearance may create questions about its skills and qualifications. In general, the approach of listing lots of services and taking an "I'll do anything" attitude is not very professional. It is not very effective at getting new clients, and it may actually deter potential clients and prompt them to look elsewhere.

Most new home-based bookkeeping businesses provide some or all of the services in the following categories:

- Bookkeeping or accounting services—monthly services, quarterly check-ups, or write-up services
- Payroll services
- Tax return preparation
- QuickBooks (or Peachtree) setup, training, consulting, and troubleshooting
- Consulting and advisory services (which can cover a wide variety of services based on the client's needs)
- Compilations, reviews, or audits, if appropriate for CPA firms. (However, many small businesses do not need or want these services unless required by a bank or other third party. Investigate the cost of liability insurance and peer review before you decide to offer these services. Many CPAs have successful accounting practices without providing these services.)

These categories are sufficient for the client to realize the types of services that you provide. Consider possible services based on your education, work experience, and interests. For example, if you do not have the training or experience in tax preparation, then you should not provide this service.

Methods to Get Started

You can use a few different methods to start your home-based bookkeeping business. Which method you choose depends on your personal situation concerning time and money.

Start from Scratch

Many people start their home-based business from scratch. This method takes the longest time to get going and build up a steady stream of income and clients. However, it is also the cheapest method to get started with the least amount of risk. Starting slowly with a smaller client base allows you to learn along the way and modify your plan as needed.

Purchase an Existing Business

The fastest method to get started is to purchase an existing business. With this method you usually purchase an existing client base (with a revenue stream) and perhaps the business name, which may help with name recognition. Usually some clients will leave during this transition stage, so expect some client attrition after the purchase. This method requires you to find a business for sale that would work as a home-based business for you. It also requires more financial resources, although you may get the owner to finance the sale based on the future billings of the business. This method has more risk because you will most likely sign a binding contract with the seller (you should have an attorney review the contract). You will be running the business right away, so there is no—or little—chance to learn and grow into the business. If you have the experience, then you may be ready for it. Otherwise, it might be too much too quickly for some people.

Purchase a Franchise

Another way to get started is to purchase a bookkeeping (or tax) franchise. When you purchase a franchise, it is like a "business in a box." You get an operating model and procedures, marketing support, a logo and name recognition, and more. This method can help you speed up the process of getting started; however, you still have the lengthy process of getting clients. Plus, this method can be quite costly. Some franchise fees are $25,000 or more, and then you have to pay ongoing royalties and advertising fees. Buying a franchise has more financial requirements and risks. You should carefully evaluate what you receive for your money and the costs versus the

Marketing after Buying a Business

I was fortunate when I started up. I bought an ongoing business that I had worked for off and on for nine years (the business was sixteen years old when I bought it). But it was 1991, and we were in the midst of a downturn in the economy similar to today's. In uncertain economic times, your business cards and word-of-mouth advertising are your best allies. I keep business cards in my purse and my car, and now that my daughters are in their twenties, each has a stack, too (and, yes, they do hand them out). When I started out, I lived in a neighborhood with lots of local stores that I frequented. Without pushing, I let them know what I did and left my card. I ended up getting a few clients from them, and some referred me to friends, which is just as good.

Nancy Gomez, CB, The Bottom Line,
www.bottomline-sb.com, Santa Barbara, CA

benefits. I would also recommend having a lawyer review the franchise agreement before you sign anything.

When deciding which method is right for you, consider several aspects: Are you still employed and starting this business part-time on the side? Are you in the planning stages and want to start at some point in the future? Have you lost your job and need to get going quickly? Do you have the financial resources to purchase a business or franchise? Do you want to minimize your risk or go full throttle and do not mind taking a financial risk? Only you can decide which method is right for you.

03 Writing a Business Plan

You might think you do not need to write a business plan to start a home-based bookkeeping business. Many people think they need only a written business plan if they plan to seek external funding. But that is not the case. You should invest the time and energy in a business plan regardless of whether you need financing or not because a plan will help guide you through the process and keep you on track along the way.

When I started my home-based accounting business many years ago, I did not write a business plan. If I had written a business plan, I think it would have helped me to avoid some mistakes and achieve success sooner. When you go through the process of writing a plan, no matter how formal or informal, it forces you to consider many aspects that you might overlook otherwise. During the process of writing the business plan, you research and analyze the industry, your competitors, your own strengths and weaknesses, and other external factors, such as political and economic conditions. The insight and knowledge gained by doing the research and analysis help you to be more informed and to make better business decisions, particularly because your vision is already written out for you. The plan will help you when you communicate with family and friends about your business, with potential clients, and with potential networking groups. It helps with your self-confidence and conveys that to others.

Writing a business plan helps you to clarify your business goals, anticipate challenges, and develop an effective marketing strategy and guides your decision making. You can improve your odds of success with your business by taking the time to write out a plan. Keep in mind that if you are not seeking external funding, it does not need to be that formal nor take too much time. Many individual parts of the business plan, such as marketing strategies, will be discussed in detail in later chapters.

Tools and Resources for Writing the Plan

Numerous tools and resources can help you write a business plan. Seminars and workshops are dedicated to this topic. Check with your local Small Business Development Center, Service Corps of Retired Executives office, or other organizations to see if they offer seminars on writing a business plan. Many SBDC and SCORE offices provide free advice to people wanting to start a business (see sidebar for more information). Contact them for an appointment to get help with your business plan. They can provide information and resources, review your plan, and guide you as you write it. Best of all, consulting with them is usually free! (If you sign up for a seminar or workshop, a fee may be required.)

Small Business Development Center and SCORE

The U.S. Small Business Administration administers the Small Business Development Center (SBDC) Program. Sixty-three lead SBDC offices (at least one in every state) have more than nine hundred service offices. Usually a service office is associated with a local community college or university or other organization. You can use the SBDC locator here: www.sba.gov/aboutsba/sbaprograms/sbdc/sbdclocator/index.html.

This is the mission of the SBDC:

"The Office of Small Business Development Centers (SBDC) provides management assistance to current and prospective small business owners. SBDCs offer one-stop assistance to individuals and small businesses by providing a wide variety of information and guidance in central and easily accessible branch locations. The program is a cooperative effort of the private sector, the educational community and federal, state, and local governments and is an integral component of Entrepreneurial Development's network of training and counseling services."

Another great resource is Service Corps of Retired Executives (www.score.org). It is a useful resource for free and confidential small business advice. When I started my business in 1991, I utilized SCORE. I met with a SCORE counselor, used the resources in its library, and thought it was a valuable resource.

Many free online resources are available to help you write your business plan as well. The Small Business Administration has online workshops, outlines of how to write your plan, and other helpful resources on its website, www.sba.gov/small businessplanner/plan/writeabusinessplan/index.html. The SCORE webpage, www .score.org/template_gallery.html, offers a free business plan template in Word to make it even easier to write your business plan.

You can look at many sample business plans for examples and guidance when you're ready to write your own. Business Plan Pro provides a sample business plan for an accounting and bookkeeping business at www.bplans.com/accounting_and_bookkeeping_business_plan/executive_summary_fc.cfm.

At the end of this chapter is a sample business plan for a home-based bookkeeping business. It includes numerous rules and comments to help you write your own business plan.

I encourage you to at least take a look at some sample business plans and the resources mentioned to help you write your own plan. You may want to continue to meet with a counselor from the SBDC or SCORE office during your first year or so of your new business to tweak your plan as needed. New questions are bound to arise.

Management and Organization

The management and organization part of your plan may change as your business evolves. Even though your business may start out with just you as the management "team," it is a good idea to consider the management and organization of your business. You may need help in some areas, and the need may change as your business grows.

Start by considering the different management functions that a business requires in addition to the overall management and planning. Marketing, operations, accounting, office administration, and human resources are needed. Most likely you will perform all of these functions yourself or with the assistance of others as needed. It is helpful to consider each one to determine if you need to seek advice or assistance with some areas depending on your skills, abilities, and time available.

Overall Management and Planning

To begin with, although the management team may be just you, it is a good idea to create a board of advisors for your business. The advisory board does not need to be that formal, but it can help you make better business decisions. When you consider whom to ask to be on your advisory board, you should consider:

- Attorney
- Insurance agent
- Banker
- Other small business owners

You may want to meet with your advisory board for breakfast or lunch on a quarterly basis. An advisory board is helpful to consider ideas or get advice concerning marketing, expansion, hiring an employee, offering new services, dealing with a difficult client, or other topics. It is always helpful to hear the opinions and advice of others to help you make better business decisions.

Human Resources

When you start your business, you probably will not need employees. That situation may change as your business grows and you can no longer handle the workload by yourself. As a home-based business you should consider whether you want people to work at your home office or if you prefer a virtual office. Thanks to the Internet and technology, you can have people work remotely without physically being in the same office.

If you plan on hiring employees (on-site or remote), this area of the plan should include information on how you will recruit and select employees, compensate them, and other considerations for dealing with employees. You want to consider what education, skills, or experience you want employees to possess. How will you locate or recruit them? You may want to contact local community colleges for accounting students. Or perhaps you need administrative office help. Whatever you need, realize that many stay-at-home parents have left the corporate world and may be happy to have a home-based part-time job.

You may want to use subcontractors instead of employees. You should consider the skills, qualifications, and other characteristics that you want in a subcontractor just as if you were hiring an employee. How will you locate subcontractors? Will they be local or remote? It is a good idea to identify others with various specialties and expertise to use when the need arises.

Personally, I use other Certified ProAdvisors as subcontractors instead of hiring employees. I like the flexibility of using different people based upon the needs of the client. So, I have different people I can call upon when the need arises, and they all have different specialties. For example, I have specific people I use for retail clients with Quickbooks Point of Sale, networking and technical issues, complex inventory situations, or even data file setup and training or data entry.

Employees or Subcontractors

When it is time to hire help, it is important to understand the difference between an employee and an independent contractor (also called a "subcontractor"). When you hire employees, you must comply with payroll rules and requirements. You need to withhold federal and state income taxes, pay federal and state unemployment taxes, withhold and pay Medicare and Medicaid, and other payroll-related requirements. The reporting and filing requirements can be tedious and time-consuming. Some small business owners want to avoid paying the employer payroll taxes and the reporting and filing requirements associated with payroll, so they strive to classify people as independent contractors instead of as employees.

Uncertain Rules for 1099 Forms

The general rule for 1099s has been that businesses are required to send a 1099-Misc form to unincorporated independent contractors who were paid more than $600 for services performed during the year. (For the full requirements, go to www.irs.gov.) However, the health care bill passed in 2010 included a provision that businesses are to issue 1099-Misc forms to all businesses (including corporations) that were paid more than $600 (for products or services) during the year. (More details and a few exceptions exist—this is only a general discussion.) This provision would mean if you wrote a check to Office Depot for $1,000 for a computer, you would need to get the EIN and send Office Depot a 1099-Misc at year's end.

Right now this provision would apply to payments made in 2012. However, the additional 1099 filing requirements would create an onerous burden and tremendous amount of paperwork for businesses. Efforts to repeal and/or amend this aspect of the health care law are under way. Visit www.irs.gov to determine the current rules and requirements for 1099-Misc forms.

When an independent contractor works for you, the payroll rules do not apply. Instead, you set the person up as a vendor, and if he meets the requirements you send him a 1099 at year's end. But you do not need to withhold or pay any payroll taxes on the person. It is cheaper and easier to pay someone as an independent contractor, which is why some companies try to classify workers as such.

To reduce abuse, the IRS has been paying more attention in recent years to the misclassification of workers as independent contractors when they should be employees. Employees may file a form (Form SS-8 Determination of Worker Status for Purposes of Federal Employment Taxes and Income Tax Withholding) asking the IRS to determine their status. Plus, a worker who is disgruntled or wants to apply for unemployment can easily file this form. If you misclassify someone as an independent contractor when the person should have been an employee, the mistake can be costly.

If the IRS determines that a worker was really an employee and not an independent contractor, then the business will be liable for payroll taxes (Medicare, Social Security, unemployment taxes) plus penalties and interest. The penalties can be 100 percent of the taxes owed if the IRS determines that the misclassification was intentional.

So how do you determine if someone is an employee or independent contractor? You should consider some general characteristics. The IRS has "20 Questions" (see pages 28–29) to help determine the proper classification of a worker. The IRS will evaluate the totality of the circumstances. Even if a worker agrees (and maybe even signs something to that effect) to be classified as an independent contractor, that fact does not carry much weight in the determination. In one case the employer had workers form an LLC to give the appearance of being independent contractors. However, based on the totality of the circumstances and the "20 Questions," they were deemed to be employees.

As the bookkeeper or accountant for small businesses, you must inform your clients about the rules and requirements. Share the "20 Questions" with them and discuss the risks and penalties for misclassifying a worker as an independent contractor instead of an employee. The penalties and interest can be substantial enough to cause a company to go out of business.

Accounting and Office Administration

When you are starting, you probably will not need help with administration or accounting functions. However, as your business grows, you may find that you

IRS 20 Questions

How to determine if a worker is an independent contractor or employee:

1. Is the worker required to comply with instructions about when, where, and how the work is done?
2. Is the worker provided training that would enable him/her to perform a job in a particular method or manner?
3. Are the services provided by the worker an integral part of the business's operations?
4. Must the services be rendered personally?
5. Does the business hire, supervise, or pay assistants to help the worker on the job?
6. Is there a continuing relationship between the worker and the person for whom the services are performed?
7. Does the recipient of the services set the work schedule?
8. Is the worker required to devote his/her full time to the person he/she performs services for?
9. Is the work performed at the place of business of the company or at specific places set by the company?
10. Does the recipient of the services direct the sequence in which the work must be done?
11. Are regular oral or written reports required to be submitted by the worker?
12. Is the method of payment hourly, weekly, monthly (as opposed to commission or by the job)?
13. Are business and/or traveling expenses reimbursed?
14. Does the company furnish tools and materials used by the worker?
15. Has the worker failed to invest in equipment or facilities used to provide the services?
16. Does the arrangement put the person in a position of realizing either a profit or loss on the work?
17. Does the worker perform services exclusively for the company rather than working for a number of companies at the same time?

18. Does the worker in fact make his/her services regularly available to the general public?
19. Is the worker subject to dismissal for reasons other than nonperformance of the contract specifications?
20. Can the worker terminate his/her relationship without incurring a liability for failure to complete the job?

For more detailed information, refer to the IRS website or IRS training materials (www.irs.gov/pub/irs-utl/emporind.pdf).

would like someone to answer the phones, reply to e-mails, or do other administrative tasks. Numerous virtual assistants now can work remotely if you need this type of help.

You need to establish an accounting system for your business. How will you track your time? Will you invoice clients, and how often? Or will you collect a retainer up front? Will you accept credit card payments? These are some basic decisions that need to be made about your accounting policies and procedures and they are discussed further in chapter 9.

Services Provided

In the business plan you should specify the purpose of the services that you will provide and identify the features and the benefits. It is important to identify the benefits that you provide for clients up front so you can include those in your marketing materials and when you talk with others about your services. Features tell about the services you provide, but benefits sell—that is why clients purchase your services. You should focus on the benefits for clients. Some benefits for businesses and business owners include:

- Improve profits or sales
- Attract new customers
- Save time
- Improve efficiency
- Pursue opportunities

- Be respected in the community and by peers
- Reduce stress and worry
- Reduce costs (save money)
- Avoid wasting time
- Avoid threats
- Avoid tasks that are undesirable
- Avoid discomfort
- Avoid embarrassment

You should also consider limitations to the services you provide. You may not have the experience or qualifications to perform some services or projects. You should acknowledge your limitations and not accept work that is beyond your capabilities. Have a referral network of other accountants and bookkeepers as needed.

Marketing

Many people hear the word *marketing* and think of advertising, but marketing is so much more than just advertising. To start with, you should research and gain a better understanding of the industry. What are the current size and trends in accounting and bookkeeping? Is the industry growing or shrinking nationally, regionally, and locally? How is technology changing the industry?

When you start your business, you need to do a lot of marketing-oriented tasks. You need a business name, logo, business cards, a website, a Facebook page, Twitter account, LinkedIn profile, and more, particularly as social media groups and technology progress. You need to devote the time and resources to get your initial brand set up to provide a professional appearance for your business. Often the website or business card may be a potential client's first impression of your business. You want the first impression to be a good, professional impression; otherwise, the client may look for someone else.

Do you have the skills and abilities to create a logo, website, and more for your business? If not, you need to budget and plan for some assistance in these areas. Maybe you need help creating a logo or a website for your business. You do not need to spend thousands of dollars, but you should consider spending several hundred dollars to get started with a basic logo and site.

You should plan on investing time to attend business luncheons, meetings, and other networking events in your area. The most effective marketing method for accounting professionals is referrals. You cultivate referrals by building relationships with other people, including attorneys, bankers, insurance agents, and other business owners. This is something you need to do personally, so you should plan on the time and money for these events.

Know Your Competition

As you develop a business plan for your bookkeeping business, it is beneficial to know as much as possible about your competition. Understanding your competition can show you how to clarify the services you will offer, how to differentiate yourself from them, and how to position your business. You want to identify the competition, research it, and analyze its strengths and weaknesses.

Identify Direct and Indirect Competitors

The first step is to identify direct and indirect competitors. Direct competitors are other bookkeeping or accounting firms providing essentially the same services that you will provide. Identify direct competitors who are located near you. Also identify direct competitors who provide services remotely and compete online.

Indirect competition includes other businesses that offer some of the same services as you. For example, indirect competition will most likely include businesses that specialize in providing tax preparation or payroll services. Indirect competition also includes substitutes for your services. For example, small business owners could do the monthly bookkeeping themselves or have a friend or relative do it. This would be a substitute for hiring you to do the bookkeeping.

To identify your direct and indirect competitors, you will need to do some research. You can use Google, the Yellow Pages, or something similar to identify local competitors. Another option is to use ReferenceUSA to search for direct competitors. On pages 105–7 is an article about how to create a mailing or contact list using ReferenceUSA. You can follow the same method to research and identify direct and indirect competitors.

Key Competitive Factors

Competitive factors are those factors that customers expect from a company and consider when choosing between competitors. Competitive factors can include price, quality, convenience, brand name, and service. It is important to identify which competitive factors are important for accounting, bookkeeping, and tax services.

Which factors are important to small business owners when they are choosing an accounting professional? Keep in mind that in many cases they will look for these factors in you personally because you are the business. Some competitive factors include:

- Being trustworthy and ethical
- Being reliable and dependable
- Being timely
- Being accurate
- Being personable
- Being convenient
- Being available
- Being reputable
- Having expertise
- Having good credentials
- Offering good rates or fees
- Providing good service or treatment

Small business owners will expect all of the factors to be met at a basic level. You should try to identify which factors will be most important to the type of client you want to target. For example, if you are targeting a niche that requires more skill and expertise, then the clients may be more concerned with expertise, credentials, and reputation. On the other hand, small, service-based businesses may be more concerned with availability, convenience, and reliability. Identifying which competitive factors are important to potential clients can help you create a competitive advantage and differentiate yourself.

Competitive Analysis

Identify the top three (or whatever number you choose) direct and indirect competitors and the key competitive factors to use for a competitive analysis. You will research these competitors and identify the services they provide. You should evaluate their strengths and weaknesses and assess how well they provide the key competitive factors. To research the competitors, you should visit their website, look for articles, reviews, or comments posted online, read their blog, look at any ads or brochures, and ask other people about them. Google the business name with different keywords, including *complaints*, *unhappy*, and others. You want to evaluate competitors' strengths and weaknesses to help you differentiate and position yourself.

As you perform the competitive analysis, pay attention to where a need in the marketplace may be unmet, where people are dissatisfied, or where a lack of service providers or something else would identify an opportunity for you.

Financial

The financial part of the business plan may be the easiest for you because you are starting a home-based bookkeeping business, but it will still require some time and thought. It is important to analyze the financial situation—assess your needs so you can plan accordingly. The financial part of the business plan usually includes the start-up costs and projected financial statements for three years. Because you will be home-based, I'd suggest you focus on projecting an income statement and not worry about the balance sheet. You may not need to project the statement of cash flows either unless you anticipate more expenses such as for hiring help.

Start-Up Costs

Start by estimating the start-up costs and how much you will need to start your business. The good news is that start-up costs for a home-based bookkeeping business do not usually add up to a significant amount of money. You may already have many of the things you will need. Use this list to help you estimate the start-up costs. Start-up costs may include:

- Computer and other office equipment
- Desk and other office furniture
- Software
- Training
- Certifications
- Memberships in organizations or associations
- Business license
- Entity formation (LLC, corporation, etc.)
- Insurance
- Office supplies
- Business cards

- Website development and hosting
- Other miscellaneous

If you do not have sufficient funds for everything, identify where you can save money or postpone the expenditure. You may buy used equipment or furniture or join some associations or organizations later when you start earning some income.

Projected Financial Statements

For financial statements, normally a business plan should include a three-year projected balance sheet, income statement, and statement of cash flows. However, because you are starting a home-based bookkeeping business and presumably will not need to apply for a bank loan or other financing, I would suggest you focus on projecting the income statement. If cash flow is a concern, you should project the statement of cash flows, too.

Projecting your income will be the most challenging. First you need to define your billing rates or fees. Then estimate the number of clients for various services and the average rate of fee to apply. For example, if you estimate that monthly bookkeeping for a small service-based business (without inventory or payroll) will average $400 per month, then you would estimate how many small service-based clients you would have per month. Plus, if you will provide payroll services, you need to determine what the average fee would be multiplied by the number of clients you have for that month. See the sidebar chart (opposite) to help give you an idea of how to estimate your income. You should start with no clients and add clients slowly during the first few months and then add them more quickly the longer you are in business. There is no right or wrong answer here; I would suggest you do several scenarios—best case, worst case, and average.

Estimating your expenses is not easy either. You should try to estimate as many expenses as you can think of and include an amount for unexpected expenses. Operating expenses may include:

- Membership dues
- Website hosting
- Phone or Internet services
- Marketing or advertising
- Insurance
- Annual business license

- Conferences, training, or continuing education
- Certifications

Using Excel or another spreadsheet program, estimate your income and expenses by month for the first three years of your business. Doing this will help you manage your finances, plan for big expenditures (new computer or whatever), and set goals for yourself.

Estimating Your Income

	Monthly Bookkeeping	Weekly Payroll	Quarterly Check-ups
Fee	$400	$120	$250
Number of Clients	5	3	8
Estimated Income	$2,000/month	$360/week	$2,000/month
Estimated Annual Income	$24,000	$18,720	$8,000

Betty's Bookkeeping

BUSINESS PLAN

Business Plan Prepared By

Betty Smith

Betty's Bookkeeping

123 Main St.

Anytown, MO 12345

888-555-3333

www.bettysbookkeeping.com

Date Prepared

June, 2011

Table of Contents

Executive Summary

Venture Description

Betty's Bookkeeping will provide bookkeeping, payroll, and QuickBooks services to small businesses in the Anytown area and nationwide. Betty's is in the start-up phase and predicts slow growth during the first year.

Management and Organization Plan

Betty's Bookkeeping will form a limited liability company for the ease and liability protection. The sole owner and manager will be Betty Smith. Subcontractors will be utilized on an as-needed basis.

Marketing Plan

A large percentage of small businesses need assistance with bookkeeping, payroll, and QuickBooks. These clients must maintain accounting records and often need assistance with them. Betty's Bookkeeping will initially serve small service-based businesses. The primary marketing activities will include networking (locally and online), QuickBooks Find a ProAdvisor referral website, blog and website, referrals, and word-of-mouth.

Financial Plan

The business start-up costs are estimated to be $4,000, which will be funded from personal savings. The business is estimated to have positive cash flow and to be profitable by month six and thereafter because expenses are minimal since it is a service-based business.

Note: You can include more details in the executive summary, but it shouldn't be more than one or two pages. It is a summary of the details included in the rest of the business plan. You write the executive summary after the rest of the plan.

Management and Organization Plan

Legal Form of Business

Betty's Bookkeeping (BB) will operate as a limited liability company (LLC) in the state of Missouri. An LLC was chosen for the entity type because of its liability protection of the owner and its simplicity of formation and operation. The LLC will be taxed as a sole proprietor.

Note: State what type of entity you chose and why you selected it.

Management Team

Betty Smith will be the owner and management team. Betty has a bachelor of science degree in accountancy and is a QuickBooks Certified ProAdvisor. She has five years of experience in bookkeeping in a variety of industries.

Note: Or, you may have something like the next paragraph.

Betty earned an associate's degree in accounting from Anytown Community College. She will take the exams to earn the certified bookkeeper designation from the American Institute of Professional Bookkeepers (AIPB). She will join the ProAdvisor Program from Intuit and earn the QuickBooks Certified ProAdvisor designation within the next two months.

No future management positions are anticipated at this time.

Note: Include details from your past as well as your future plans along with estimated dates of completion or graduation.

Your education may include:

- Bookkeeping or accounting classes—may include courses such as those of Penn Foster
- Associate's degree (two years)
- Bachelor's degree (four years)

- Master's degree (five plus years)

- Certifications or credentials may include:

- Certified bookkeeper (from AIPB)

- QuickBooks Certified ProAdvisor (from Intuit)

- Certified tax professional (from National Association of Tax Professionals)

- Payroll (from American Payroll Association)

- Certified public accountant (AICPA and state boards of accountancy)

- Enrolled agent

Advisory Board

An advisory board will be formed to help the owner analyze situations and plan a strategy for the future. The advisory board will meet quarterly unless a need to meet more frequently arises. No formal compensation will be provided for the advisory board. However, the meals for all meetings will be provided as well as "thank you" gifts at year-end. Advisory board members will be sought with the following areas of expertise: banking, legal, insurance, marketing, general business experience, and the client's perspective.

> **Note:** Whom do you know who could help provide advice to you as needed? If you cannot think of anyone right now, go ahead and list the area of expertise but, instead of a name, indicate "To Be Determined."

Recruitment and Selection of Employees

Currently Betty has no plans to hire employees. Should the need arise when additional help or specialization is needed, subcontractors will be utilized on an as-needed basis. Subcontractors will be identified from networking and building relationships with other accounting professionals locally, online, and at seminars or conferences.

Subcontractors will be selected based on their experience and qualifications, reliability and dependability, availability, and quality of work performed. The owner will develop and maintain a list of potential subcontractors (or others for referrals) for areas of additional specialization in the event that a client has needs beyond the owner's current capabilities.

Compensation and Ownership

Betty is the founder and 100 percent owner of the business. Initially all money will be retained in the business to cover expenses for education, training, certifications, memberships, and other start-up expenses. As the business grows, Betty will take owner's draws from the business as cash flow permits.

Communication

The company's value and expectations will be displayed and reviewed periodically. Communication will be via e-mail, instant messaging, and phone.

Infrastructure

Key advisors will be sought from the following specialists: lawyers, bankers, insurance agents, computer specialists (IT), tax accountants, and others as needed.

Service Plan

Purpose of Service

Many small business owners need assistance with their bookkeeping and accounting. The IRS requires them to maintain adequate records, and they must file tax returns annually. So bookkeeping and accounting services are necessary for most small businesses. Many small business owners do not have enough time or accounting knowledge to do the bookkeeping themselves. However, some of them will enter daily transactions on their own (usually into QuickBooks). These clients usually need QuickBooks setup, training, troubleshooting, and other services. Plus, they may request monthly assistance with bank reconciliations or other tasks.

Betty's Bookkeeping will provide accounting and bookkeeping services as follows:

- Monthly bookkeeping services
- Payroll services
- QuickBooks setup and training

- QuickBooks troubleshooting and consulting
- QuickBooks tune-ups
- Other bookkeeping services

Features and Benefits

The features provided by Betty's Bookkeeping are the services listed above. However, clients will be more interested in the benefits provided, such as:

- Reduce stress and worry (confidence that the work will be done right)
- Improve profits or sales (timely reports)
- Save time (information and reports readily available)
- Improve efficiency (information readily available)
- Pursue opportunities (identify best-selling items or most profitable customers)
- Reduce costs (save money, avoid penalties)
- Avoid threats (for late payments)
- Avoid tasks that are undesirable (bookkeeping tasks)
- Avoid discomfort (worrying about bookkeeping)
- Avoid embarrassment (from late payments)

> **Note:** Keep in mind that "features tell, but benefits sell": Features tell about the services you provide. Clients buy the benefits you provide. Sell the benefits.

Service Limitations

Betty's Bookkeeping will not provide tax preparation services and will develop a network of other accounting professionals who provide tax preparation services.

Betty's Bookkeeping will not accept clients with complex accounting needs such as manufacturing companies, large contractors that require certified payroll, and other specialized needs.

Betty's Bookkeeping may decline to accept some clients for a variety of reasons when deemed necessary (for ethical, moral, or other reasons).

Service Liability

Some liabilities exist when providing bookkeeping services. In the event of a mistake or missed deadline, the client may incur penalties and/or interest. Betty's Bookkeeping will be responsible for any penalties and interest due to a mistake Betty made.

Betty will not have check-signing authority on any client bank accounts to avoid any related liability issues.

Some liability issues may exist concerning computer systems, and due care and procedures will be followed to ensure adequate backup.

Betty's Bookkeeping will ensure adequate security of client records and information to prevent loss electronically or physically.

Betty's Bookkeeping will obtain errors and omissions insurance to cover the services provided. Betty will use engagement letters, checklists, and guides to minimize risks.

> **Note:** Identify the liabilities, related insurance requirements (and costs), and what you can do to minimize the liability. You would probably include more details than are provided as an example here.

Operations

Operating procedures will vary based upon client needs and circumstances. Betty will strive to work remotely and online with most clients utilizing available technology for efficient processes.

> **Note:** You should document your ideal workflow and alternatives for different client needs. Create and utilize checklists and forms to help manage the work and to ensure that tasks or due dates are not overlooked. You may want to modify the examples provided throughout the book to meet your needs.

Facilities
Betty's Bookkeeping will be a home-based business.

Related Products/Services and Spin-offs
Betty's business may provide training seminars or webinars in the future.

Governmental Approvals
Betty's Bookkeeping will register the business with the local, city, and state government agencies as appropriate.

> **Note:** If you will provide tax services, you need to register and obtain a Prepare Tax Identification Number and comply with various rules and regulations for tax practitioners.

If you are a certified public accountant, you need to comply with the rules and regulations of the state board of accountancy and the AICPA.

If you are not a CPA, you should still check with the state board of accountancy for the rules on using the word *accountant* or *accounting* because some states have strict guidelines on who can use these words.

Marketing Plan

Industry Profile
Current Size
Betty's Bookkeeping would be in the industry of "other accounting services," which includes bookkeepers and accountants other than CPAs. It does not include firms that provide tax preparation services only or payroll services only (they are classified separately).

The 2007 Economic Census (per the U.S. Census Bureau using Fact Finder) provides the following industry statistics. Other related industries are included for comparison and informative proposes.

NAICS Code	Title	Number of U.S. Businesses	Revenues (in billions)
541211	Offices of CPAs	57,602	$66.58
541213	Tax preparation services	24,911	5.25
541214	Payroll services	4,842	28.92
541219	Other accounting services (includes bookkeepers and accountants other than CPAs)	36,011	13.36

Additional information from the 2007 Economic Census provides the number of firms based on number of employees. As the chart below shows, about 36 percent have one employee, and about 73 percent have four or fewer employees. Only 11 percent of the firms have ten or more employees.

Firms Based on Number of Employees

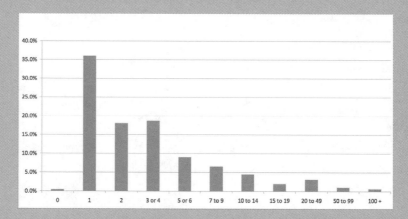

Growth Potential

The accounting industry is relatively stable, with little or no growth. Businesses need accounting and bookkeeping services whether the economy is good or bad, although they may try to minimize their costs during a downturn in the economy. Increases in the number of businesses should help provide increases for the accounting services industry, too.

Industry Trends

The biggest changes in the industry of other accounting services recently have been the result of changes in technology. Improvements in the speed and availability of the Internet have created more opportunities for working with clients remotely. Additionally, clients are more comfortable doing tasks online—from shopping to paying bills online via their bank to social networking as with Facebook. These changes have created opportunities to work more collaboratively with clients and to improve workflow and efficiency.

Other Characteristics

The accounting services industry is somewhat seasonal in nature. A lot of work may be available right before and after year-end as businesses need to finish up their accounting for the year and prepare to file their income taxes. Additionally, the beginning of the year is busy as many small businesses implement new accounting systems and procedures for the upcoming year.

Competitive Analysis

Direct Competition

Based on research of the local area, the following direct competitors were identified.

- Bob's Bookkeeping and Tax—located in Anytown, provides bookkeeping, QuickBooks, and tax preparation services but not payroll.
- Other direct competitors identified from your research
- Other direct competitors operating online

Note: Use ReferenceUSA, Google, and the Yellow Pages to identify local competitors. Determine which are the most direct competitors based on the services you will offer and the types of clients you anticipate).

Indirect Competition

Indirect competition includes CPA firms that may offer bookkeeping services as well as small business owners (or their friends, family, or others) who do it themselves. Some bookkeeping services operating online outsource the bookkeeping to other countries. These companies usually offer lower rates.

> **Note:** You should do some research and consider other ways small businesses can get their bookkeeping done.

Future Competition

Starting a business that offers bookkeeping services is easy, and the start-up costs are relatively minimal. Requirements or barriers to entry are minimal, which means new competitors can easily enter the industry.

Competitive Analysis

In this section list your main competitors (direct, indirect, or both), the key competitive factors, and an assessment of the strengths and weaknesses of the competitors. Provide an honest assessment from the perspective of a potential client. How do you compare with the competitors? Look for advantages or disadvantages to help identify potential problem areas or areas for improvement.

Market Analysis

Target Market Profile

Betty's Bookkeeping will focus on small service-based businesses, including companies in the following industries:

- Lawn and landscape
- Plumbing
- Electrical
- HVAC
- Handyman
- Home remodeling

- Painting
- Wedding planning
- Event organizing
- Other service-based businesses

> **Note:** Using ReferenceUSA, you can identify potential clients and research how many potential clients might be in a certain area. See the article on pages 105–7 for details on how to search the database.

Client Profile

Initially Betty's Bookkeeping will target clients with one to ten employees in the Anytown area in the following industries—plumbing, electrical, and HVAC.

> **Note:** Identify the types of clients you want to target, including the details about the type of business, the industry, their size, and more.

Future Markets

In the future Betty's Bookkeeping may pursue more professionals, such as engineers, architects, and attorneys.

Pricing

Pricing Strategy

Betty's Bookkeeping will be priced competitively with an initial hourly rate of $60. After Betty becomes a QuickBooks Certified ProAdvisor, the rate will increase to $65 per hour, and after she earns the Certified Bookkeeper designation, the rate will increase to $70 per hour.

Initially the normal billing rate will be reduced to $50 per hour for the first three months to help obtain the first few clients. Clients will be informed that the billing rate is discounted and that it will increase after the initial three months.

Price List

Betty's Bookkeeping will provide some fixed-fee services for quarterly QuickBooks tune-ups, payroll services, and more. However, the actual rates for these fixed-fee services have not yet been determined.

Note: Providing some fixed-fee services is a good idea because they can help improve your profitability. However, you probably will not know what the prices should be when you are starting the business. After you have some experience, you should have a better idea of how to set these prices.

Market Penetration

Company Image

Betty's Bookkeeping will present a professional image at all times—including in dress (business casual) and appearance, website, client communications (both written and oral), and business cards. Betty will strive to convey a casual and open attitude to encourage clients to feel comfortable and relaxed.

Client Service

Betty's Bookkeeping will strive to provide outstanding client service by responding to all calls or e-mails within twenty-four hours (twelve hours when possible). She will complete work as promised in a timely manner and answer quick questions when they arise.

Internet

Betty's Bookkeeping will have a website with a professional appearance and a blog. Betty will strive to blog regularly to keep content updated and changing. Betty will utilize social media to develop online presence, name recognition, networking, and relationships. Initially Betty will use LinkedIn, a Facebook page for the business, and Twitter. In the future (six to twelve months), Betty will create short video tips about QuickBooks and other topics to post on YouTube and in blog posts.

Advertising and Promotion

Traditional mass media advertising (ads in newspapers, magazines, etc.) will not be utilized. Small ads may be placed in newsletters for nearby neighborhoods, churches, schools, etc. Betty will order some merchandise with the QuickBooks logo (shirt, hat, etc.) to wear at various places (grocery store, post office, Little League games, etc.) to prompt people to ask questions.

Telemarketing/Direct Mail

Betty's Bookkeeping does not plan to use telemarketing and direct mail at this time.

Financial Plan

Start-Up Costs

Betty's Bookkeeping already has many items for the home office that will be utilized and help minimize start-up costs. Start-up costs are estimated as follows:

Computer and other office equipment: Need scanner	$500
Desk and other office furniture: Need a lamp, chair mat, miscellaneous	100
Software: Join QuickBooks ProAdvisor Program	500
Certifications: AIPB, Certified ProAdvisor included with membership	500
Memberships: AIPB, ProAdvisor program listed above	30
Business license	50
Entity formation: Filing fees with state	200
Insurance: E&O and riders on homeowner's insurance	500
Office supplies	50

Business cards	50
Website development and hosting	100
Other miscellaneous	200
Total Estimated Start-up Costs	$2,780

Sales Projections

Sales are projected to be $25,000 the first year, $50,000 the second year, and $85,000 the third year.

Note: These projections will require some time and assumptions. You can do some calculations such as the service provided (monthly bookkeeping, payroll, Quick-Books setup and training, etc.) times the estimated number of clients (increasing gradually each month—slowly at first but then more quickly over time) times the estimated average fee.

Income Projections

Net income is projected to be $15,000 for the first year, $40,000 for the second year, and $75,000 for the third year.

Note: These projections will require more time and assumptions. You will need to estimate expenses for the next three years to calculate the net income.

Cash Requirements

Betty's Bookkeeping will need $4,000 cash to start the business and operate for the first few months.

Note: Estimate how much cash you will need to cover start-up costs and the first few months of operations. Add a little cushion to be safe. If you are the sole provider for yourself or others, then you should consider personal expenses and financial needs as well.

Sources of Financing

Betty has personal savings, which will be used to fund the start-up of the business.

> **Note:** If you need to borrow money to get started, indicate the source of the funds and when the money will be repaid.

Projected Financial Statements

Monthly Cash Flow Report (for three years)

Year-end Income Statement

Year-end Balance Sheet

Ratio Analysis

> **Note:** Typically these are the financial statements included with a business plan. However, because this is a home-based business that does not require outside financing or funding (presumably), then you can leave out the balance sheet, ratio analysis, and maybe the cash flow report.

After you have decided that you are ready to start your own business, you need to do some things to establish your business.

What's in a Name?

What will the name of your business be? That sounds like an easy question, but coming up with a business name can be quite difficult. The two most common options are: come up with a business name that clearly establishes your business's identity, or use your own name to start the business.

One caveat: Picking the right name is much more important now than in the past due to the advent of Internet, search engines, social media, and more. Changing your name in the middle of your growing business could lose you the recognition and viral momentum of your business name. Some brand confusion could develop, and clients could be scared off. Online links and URLs will no longer work, and you will lose momentum you may have had with the search engines such as Google. Some clients, contacts, acquaintances, and others will have your old e-mail address and have difficulty locating you. You really lose a lot when you have to rebrand your business both online and offline, which makes selecting the right business name an important decision.

Characteristics of a Good Business Name

Close your eyes for a minute and think about some business names in your community or online. You can probably name a few that are good. What do you think makes a good business name? What about those names that make you wonder, "What were they thinking?"? What is wrong with them? Sometimes common sense and instinct can help you identify a good business name. For years I knew I didn't have the right name for my business. Now "Long for

What Not to Do When Naming Your Business

When I started my business, I was in a hurry to get the business started. I was not really sure what services I would be providing because the services depended on what my clients needed. I had trouble coming up with a good name that would properly identify my business because my business's identity had yet to be established. I wound up using my own name (Michelle L. Long, CPA). I was never very happy with it, but I could no longer wait to come up with a good business name—I needed to get my business started.

Many years later I decided to change my business entity type from a sole proprietor to an LLC (see discussion of entities later in this chapter), and yet I still could not come up with a good name for my business. I was no longer providing traditional accounting services, and I was doing much more consulting and training. I tried to come up with a business name without much luck. Finally I decided on "M. Long Consulting, LLC" ("Long Consulting" was already taken) for lack of a better name, but I wasn't completely happy with it.

After a few more years with a business name I didn't like, an opportunity came up from Intuit. Intuit frequently had online webinars and events, and it was going to allow me to use its platform. I would be able to have online meetings or events to discuss growing your business and other topics for QuickBooks users and accounting professionals. Intuit was going to have several people from various businesses doing events, so I needed to come up with a name for mine. I knew that "M. Long Consulting" would not be a good name for it. However, I wanted a name that would tie in with my business and my brand to help with my own marketing. I asked the people at Intuit if they could help brainstorm ideas for a name for me. I told them the topics I thought I would like to discuss in the room and asked them to see what they could come up with for a name.

Finally the suggestion for a name came: "Long for Success." My first thought was that it was a cute play on my last name but that it was too cheesy for an accounting professional. However, the more I thought about it, the more I realized that I'm not providing traditional accounting services anymore. The name actually worked well for the type of services I wanted to provide, and it was more catchy and memorable than my previous business names. The real clincher was when I

> discovered that the URL was available for my website. Finally, after about eighteen years in business, I had a real business name!
>
> Lessons learned:
>
> - ■ Picking a business name can be difficult.
>
> - ■ Seek the help of others to come up with a business name.
>
> - ■ You must choose a name to start the business. Put some time and energy into selecting a good business name from the beginning.
>
> - ■ You can change the name later—but not changing the name is preferable. You face many challenges to your brand when you change the business name.

Success, LLC" just feels right for my business. You want to strive for a name for your business that is good, memorable, and meaningful.

Dedicate some time to selecting your business name. Consider these characteristics of a good business name:

- ■ It is not too long—"Betty's Bookkeeping, Payroll, Taxes, and Other Accounting Services" is too long. If the name is too long, clients won't remember the whole name; it will be a long website address (which people may type incorrectly); and it just takes too long to say in conversations with others.
- ■ It is easy to say and spell—you don't want people to have difficulty pronouncing your name or spelling it. If they misspell it, then it is harder for them to search for you online or to remember your website or e-mail address.
- ■ It relates to your type of business and services—this may or may not work for you. If you provide a variety of services, it is more difficult to narrow them down for the name. Plus, you may not want to limit yourself or define your services too much because your business may evolve over time. I definitely do not provide the same services now as I provided when I started my business.
- ■ It is unique within your industry—when it comes to bookkeeping or accounting services, this factor is more challenging. I know numerous

businesses across the country with a name that includes "Bottom Line" in some form. You can use Google to help you see what names are already being used.

- It is somewhat creative—many accounting professionals (myself included) are not very creative. So, don't be afraid to seek the assistance of others to help you select a business name.
- It represents your brand and image—consider the image you want for your business. Some names may not be suitable for one reason or another.
- It is not trendy—hopefully you will be in business for a long time, so you should avoid a trendy name.

You will find it difficult to come up with a name that has all of these characteristics. These are just some guidelines to help guide you in selecting a name. These are not hard and fast rules.

What Services Will You Provide?

When selecting a business name, start by considering the services you plan to offer. Often you will read that the business name should convey the type of work or services you offer. This rule might work for plumbers, electricians, and others, but it is much more difficult when you are providing accounting and bookkeeping services.

Consider: Are you going to provide just bookkeeping services? Will you provide payroll services as well? What about tax preparation? Will you provide QuickBooks consulting and training? Plus, you should consider what types of services you will provide in three to five years or more so the business name will still be applicable. Make a list of all the services you might initially provide and a list of those you might consider in the future.

Naming Legalities

Some states will not allow you to use the word *accounting* or *accountant* in your name or business description unless you are a certified public accountant. You should check with your state board of accountancy to see what the rules are for your state. You do not want to start your business and find out a year or two later that you must change your name due to this legality.

Create a List of Possible Names

Now it is time to start brainstorming; list a lot of different ideas as they come to you, regardless of how farfetched or cheesy they may sound. Do not critique or analyze them yet. Instead, just list a bunch of possibilities and different variations. Consider a play on your name or a motto that works for what you're offering. You may want to get others to help you brainstorm as well.

It is best to wait a day before you start narrowing the list. Let the list sink in a bit, and be sure to give each name careful thought. Start by eliminating names that just do not work well for one reason or another, be it that the name is too long or that it simply doesn't make sense for the services you're offering. Keep cutting names until you get down to about ten names that you will investigate as possibilities.

Investigate Possible Names

Now that you have a list of possible names, investigate them further. You should check several factors:

- Name availability in your state: Go to the Secretary of State's website and do a business name search to see if the name is already taken. Also investigate the rules in your state for business names on the website for the secretary of state. For example, usually corporations must include "Inc.," "Corporation," "Corp.," etc. in their name. Limited liability companies usually must include "LLC," "L.L.C.," etc.

- Domain names: Search to see if that website name is available in the domain .com. If it is not available, is there something close, possibly with some abbreviations? Finding an available domain name may be the most difficult aspect of your search. If the domain name you want is not available, go to the website to check it out. Is it really a website, or is it being parked (i.e., it has a lot of links or ads on it, indicating someone bought it for the name only)? Some people buy a lot of domain names and then try to sell them to others. If it has been parked, then you may want to consider buying the domain name. You can do some research to identify the domain name owner. If it is the name you want, then it may be worth buying the domain name to get a .com domain. This could cost you a few hundred dollars. If you cannot get a .com domain, then look for a name with .net, .biz, or .us, but understand that .com is preferable. If the domain name you want is available, buy it now. You can work on the website later, but it's best to secure the domain name early to prevent it from being snatched up.

After you weed through this criterion you may be down to just one or two names on your list of possibles, or you may have no more names on your list. If the latter is the case, then it is time to go back to your original full list of names and consider other names or variations and try again. It may be beneficial to have others help you select your business name. I never could come up with a good name for my business, but some creative people came up with a great name for my business.

Getting Legal

After you have selected your business name, the next step is to determine which type of entity is right for your business. Your personal financial situation and tax implications should be considered. I recommend you seek legal advice for this decision. The information below can help you begin to understand the different types of entities with a listing of a few general pros and cons of each type. This information can help you be prepared to ask questions and discuss the issue with your attorney and possibly a tax advisor if you are not familiar with the tax implications. This information is not intended to be legal or tax advice.

You will need to complete and file various forms with your state (such as articles of incorporation, articles of formation, registration of a fictitious name, etc.) depending on which type of business entity you select. In many states the Secretary of State's website will provide information about which forms are required for each type of entity along with the costs. Some states even provide the required documents as PDF forms that you can complete and file online (or print for your attorney to review). For example, the articles of organization for an LLC from the Missouri Secretary of State's website are included in the appendices. The filing fees, incorporation fees, etc. will vary by state and can cost from $150 to $500.

If your state does not provide the forms online, then other options are available. Online companies (MyCorporation, LegalZoom, etc.) can help you complete and file the forms with your state. You can use Google to find sample forms that you need. Finally, the public library usually has books, such as *How to Form Your Own LLC* with a CD of sample forms in it. (Or you could order the book online at www.nolo.com.) After you prepare the required documents, you may wish to have your attorney review them.

Types of Entities and Considerations

Depending on which type of entity you select, the state has different rules and requirements for naming your business. For example, if the business is a corporation, many states require "Inc.," "Corporation," "Corp," or something similar in the business name to indicate that it is a corporation. Check with your Secretary of State for the rules in your state.

Sole Proprietor

A sole proprietor is the most common form of business. You are the sole owner, and your personal assets have no liability protection of your personal assets (i.e., if someone sues the business, your personal assets are at risk, too). In general, the state has no filing requirements. If you use your own name for the business, you could simply wake up one morning and declare, "I'm in business," and you would be operating as a sole proprietor. Of course, you would need to obtain business licenses and permits, open a bank account, etc. But you do not have to file anything with the Secretary of State to form a sole proprietor as you need to do with the other business entities.

In some states if you are a sole proprietor and not using your own name as the business name, then you need to file a Registration of Fictitious Name form (or something similar). For example, if I want to operate my business as "Michelle L. Long, CPA," then I don't need to register a fictitious name because it is my own name. If my business name is "M. Long Consulting," then I need to file a Registration of Fictitious Name because it is not my name. In some states a fictitious name may be referred to as "doing business as" or "DBA." Usually the state website has a lot of information regarding this process, but call the state if you have questions. A sample of the Missouri Registration of Fictitious Name form is in the appendices.

Because you are a sole proprietor, all the profits or losses of the business will flow through to your personal tax return. You will file a Schedule C form for the business with your personal 1040 tax return. As a sole proprietor, you are not an employee, but instead you may take owner's draws from the business. If the business is profitable, you will need to make quarterly estimated tax payments and will be subject to the self-employment tax as well.

Partnership

In the event that two or more people will own the business, you may choose to operate as a partnership. Registration isn't really required, but you may need to register a fictitious name of the partnership in your state, as mentioned for sole proprietors. You should have a written partnership agreement, which you may also need to file with the state. You can find sample partnership agreements online or in books as discussed previously, but you will need to modify yours as needed. If you have two equal partners, what will you do in the event of a disagreement? It is a good idea to designate a neutral third party to be the "tie-breaker" when needed. Additional considerations will include: What if one of the partners dies? What happens to her ownership in the business? Does it automatically go to her heirs, or can the remaining partner buy them out? As you can see, you have a lot more to consider when you are forming a partnership. You should seek the advice and assistance of an attorney.

The partnership will need to file a partnership tax return (Form 1065), and the profits or losses of the business will flow through to the partners (on a Schedule K-1 form) to be included on the personal tax return of each partner. Partnership tax laws are more complex, and you may need to seek assistance from a tax professional.

Corporation (C or S)

If you decide to form a corporation, then you can get some liability protection of your personal assets. However, the liability protection will not apply if you personally guarantee business loans (which most banks and credit card companies require of a new small business), are personally negligent, or fail to pay payroll or sales taxes. You will need to file Articles of Incorporation with the Secretary of State to form the corporation. Some states require other documents to be filed initially and on an annual basis to maintain the corporation in good standing. Check with the Secretary of State to determine the requirements for your corporation.

You need to name officers of the corporation (president, vice president, secretary, and treasurer) and a board of directors (which may be just you and your spouse or significant other). You will need bylaws and annual meetings with minutes. The board of directors will need to authorize certain activities (such as borrowing money or selling an asset) and document such activities in the minutes of the board meetings. You will purchase stock of the corporation and will be paid as an employee. You probably should have an attorney to assist you with the requirements for a corporation.

A corporation is a legal entity separate from the owners. The owners of the corporation are employees, and the payroll tax rules and requirements will apply. The corporation will file a corporate tax return (Form 1120 for C corporations or Form

Provided by the law office of Richard E. Gier, PA, www.GierLaw.com

	Sole Proprietorship	General Partnership	Limited Liability Company (LLC)
Protection of Owners' Personal Assets	Owner and entity are viewed as the same for liability purposes. Owner's assets are at risk from liabilities of entity.	Partnership and its owners are liable for liabilities of entity. Every owner's assets are at risk from liabilities of entity.	Owners' assets generally not at risk for business liabilities unless owner guarantees obligations, is personally negligent in causing liability or fails to pay withheld or collected taxes. State laws may increase liability exposure.
Tax Treatment	Profits and losses not taxed to entity, but are taxed to owners on flow-through basis.	Profits and losses not taxed to entity, but are taxed to owners on flow-through basis.	One owner LLC taxed as sole proprietorship, multiple-owner LLC taxed as partnership. May elect to be taxed as corporation.
Complexity and Cost	No registration required to form. May be required to register use of fictitious name. Single owners businesses may be sole proprietorships by default if no other steps are taken.	No registration required to form. May be required to register use of fictitious name. Written Partnership Agreement should be created to govern entity and ownership rights. Partnerships may be created by default by co-owners.	Registration and filing fees required. Annual fees and taxes may apply. Operating Agreement which governs entity is required. May not be required to hold annual meetings of owners. Generally must include "LLC" or similar suffix in name.

© Richard E. Gier 2010. Information contained in Business Entity Selection Chart may vary by state and does not constitute the provision of legal advice. Consult legal counsel licensed in the state in which business entity is contemplated.

	Corporation (C-Corp)	Small Business Corporation (S-Corp)
Protection of Owners' Personal Assets	Owners' assets generally not at risk for business liabilities unless owner guarantees obligations, is personally negligent in causing liability or fails to pay withheld or collected taxes. State laws may increase liability exposure.	Owners' assets generally not at risk for business liabilities unless owner guarantees obligations, is personally negligent in causing liability or fails to pay withheld or collected taxes. State laws may increase liability exposure.
Tax Treatment	Profits and losses taxed at entity level. Dividends distributed to owners are taxed as income to owners.	Profits and losses not taxed to entity, but are taxed to owners on flow-through basis.
Complexity and Cost	Registration and filing fees required. Annual fees and taxes may apply. Bylaws and Board of Directors are required. Must hold annual meetings. Generally must include "Inc." or similar suffix in name.	Registration and filing fees required. Annual fees and taxes may apply. Bylaws and Board of Directors are required. Must hold annual meetings. Generally must include "Inc." or similar suffix in name. Ownership is restricted in number and type of shareholder. Timely election of Small Business Corporation status required.

© Richard E. Gier 2010. Information contained in Business Entity Selection Chart may vary by state and does not constitute the provision of legal advice. Consult legal counsel licensed in the state in which business entity is contemplated.

1120-S for S corporations), and the tax laws are more complex. The profits or losses of a C corporation are taxed at the corporate level.

If the corporation elects to be taxed as an S corporation, then you would need to file an Election by a Small Business Corporation (Form 2553) with the Internal Revenue Service within two months and fifteen days after the beginning of the tax year. The profits or losses of an S corporation flow through to the owners (Form K-1) to be included on the personal return of the owners. Some owners like this flow-through because many businesses have losses in the early years. For an S corporation these losses will flow through to the personal returns of the owners and offset other income. S corporations and their owners have some other tax benefits and tax-planning opportunities. However, the rules can be quite complex and are beyond the scope of this book. You should consult with your tax advisor to determine if it would be advantageous for you to form an S corporation. Keep in mind the additional costs of a corporation (annual reporting and filing requirements, payroll, and additional tax complexity compared to the possible benefits).

Limited Liability Company (LLC)

The limited liability company has become an increasingly popular choice over the past few years. A limited liability company provides some liability protection without the complexity of a corporation. With an LLC, you need to file articles of organization with the state, and you need an operating agreement. You can form a single-member LLC, which provides a good alternative to operating as a sole proprietor.

An LLC can be taxed as a sole proprietor or can elect to be taxed as an S corporation. If the LLC is taxed as a sole proprietor, then you take owner's draws and file a Schedule C form, just like a sole proprietor.

Obtain an Employer Identification Number (EIN)

After you have registered your business with the state, the next step is to obtain an employer identification number (EIN), which may be called a "tax ID number," from the Internal Revenue Service. Go to www.irs.gov to fill out the EIN application (SS-4) and obtain an EIN for your business. You need to indicate the business name and type of entity, so you cannot do this until those steps have been completed. For your benefit, the Form SS-4—Application for Employer ID Number is included in the appendices.

Even if you will operate your business as a sole proprietor with no employees, you should obtain an EIN. As a sole proprietor, if you perform services for other businesses, and they pay you over $600 during the year, those businesses will need to send you a 1099-Misc form at year's end. You will need to provide them with your EIN for this purpose. You will use your EIN to open a business checking account and to put on the business tax return as well.

Business License or Permit

After you have selected the type of entity and registered with the state, the next step is to get a business license. Many cities, counties, or states require you to obtain this license. To get your business license, contact city hall or your county government office because each will have its own requirements You will need your official business name and EIN number to apply for your business license. Keep in mind that you usually have to renew the license annually and that it may cost anywhere from $50 to several hundred dollars.

Another consideration is that some local governments now require permits for home-based businesses or that your homeowners' association may set rules and restrictions concerning home-based businesses. Contact your city hall and homeowners' association to see if these apply to you.

Sales Tax License

In most states accounting and bookkeeping services are not subject to sales taxes. However, you need to check with your state to confirm. For example, I believe that Connecticut has different rules and that the services are considered a retail sale and subject to sales taxes. I think this is probably the exception to the rule, but you need to confirm the rules in your city and state.

On the other hand, if you will sell products such as software, books, training guides, or other products, then you will probably need to collect and remit sales taxes on product sales. It is important to clarify with your city and state which sales taxes might apply to your business. You do not want to be in business for several years and then have a sales tax audit and discover that you should have been collecting sales taxes when you were not.

Business Checking Account

After you have formed your business entity and obtained an EIN, it is time to open a business checking account. You should not mix business and personal expenses for many reasons. One reason is that the Internal Revenue Service may disallow many deductions as personal if you do not keep business expenses separate. Also, if your business is a corporation and you do not operate it like a corporation, in the event of a lawsuit the plaintiffs can "pierce the corporate veil," and you lose the liability protection of the corporation. Besides, if you are going to have a business, then you should treat it like a business. Set up a separate business checking account. Many banks offer free checking to small businesses. Depending on what type of entity the business is, you can take money out of the business as an "owner's draw" or paychecks.

If you accidentally pay for business expenses with personal funds, then have the business reimburse you. Or, if there is insufficient cash in the business checking account, then you may record the business expenses as an "owner's contribution" or "due to owner" depending on the entity type. Get a business debit card to use for business expenses.

Piercing the Corporate Veil

Many people form a corporation for the liability protection of their personal assets—the "corporate veil." In other words, if someone sues the corporation, the personal assets of the shareholders (i.e., the owners) would not be at risk. It is important to maintain corporate formalities to preserve the liability protection. Otherwise, a lawyer may persuade a judge to "pierce the corporate veil" of liability protection, and the personal assets of shareholders would be at risk.

This is why it is important for a corporation to function as a corporation. It is important to keep the paperwork and filing requirements of the corporation up-to-date —the annual registration forms, minutes from the annual meeting of the board of directors, corporate minutes authorizing certain corporate actions, etc. It is important to maintain separate bank accounts for the corporation. You should not commingle business and personal funds or expenses (regardless of the entity type).

Business Credit Cards

If you decide to charge business expenses, you should obtain a credit card in the business name. Normally you have to personally guarantee or sign for the business card, but doing so helps establish credit in the business name. Plus, having a business credit card can help keep business and personal expenses separate.

If you do not want a new credit card in the business name, then you may want to use just one personal credit card for business only.

Marketing Materials

This book has a full chapter on marketing later with many more details. However, you should take a few initial steps when you establish the business.

Brand Identity

Think of some notable corporate brands, such as Target, Walmart, McDonald's, and Coca-Cola, and consider what comprises their brand. You should consider several components of a brand:

- Name (short, simple, memorable)
- Color (Target is red; McDonald's is red and yellow, etc.)
- Logo (the Target bull's-eye or the Golden Arches of McDonald's, for example)
- Fonts/script (for example, the Coca-Cola name is in a cursive font)
- Image (Target is trendy; Walmart is low cost)

For us our appearance, dress, mannerisms, e-mail signatures, phone messages, and everything about our business are all part of our brand. For now just think about what image you want for your brand. Everything you do should be consistent with that brand image in mind. For example, if you want your brand image to be professionalism, then you should not have a silly clip-art logo. That would not be consistent with a professional brand image. Write down some aspects that will define your brand and keep them in mind as you begin developing the marketing for your business.

Logo

When I started my business, I used the Certified Public Accountant logo provided by the American Institute of Certified Public Accountants (AICPA). Then, when I joined the QuickBooks ProAdvisor Program and became a Certified ProAdvisor, I began using that logo, too, alongside the CPA logo.

I never had a real company logo for my business until a few years ago. I decided I needed a logo to go with my new business name (Long for Success, LLC). I knew graphic artists could provide me with several (five to ten) possible logos. However, this service could be quite costly (i.e., from $500 to several thousand dollars), and I was concerned that five to ten possibilities would not be enough for me to find the right logo for my business.

I discovered that Intuit had partnered with an online company, 99designs, to form Intuit Creative Solutions (http://intuit.99designs.com) to help bring together designers with people like me who are looking for a logo (or other creative designs). As part of the process, you set up a logo contest by which several designers submit their ideas based upon the requirements you specify and the feedback you provide. My logo contest lasted a week, and I had about thirty designers submit over four hundred variations of logos (many were modifications and changes based on feedback from me about what I liked or did not like about them). At the end of the contest, I selected the winning design and had a logo for my business. I really liked the ability to see logos submitted by numerous designers, and best of all it was only a few hundred dollars.

You can use other ways to get a logo for your business. Perhaps you have a friend, relative, or neighbor who is creative and could help you with a logo. Contact the high school, local community college, or university to see if some students would be interested in creating a logo for you. The Nike swish was created by a graphic design student and cost Nike only $35 (many years ago, of course, but still a bargain!).

Similar to selecting a name for your business, it helps to know what makes a good logo. Again, think of some well-known logos—Nike's swish or Target's bull's-eye—and think about how their characteristics compare with these characteristics of a good logo:

- Is simple and uncluttered
- Is memorable
- Works in a variety of formats (i.e., black and white, small for Twitter, LinkedIn, or Facebook or large for webheaders)
- Represents your brand or image
- Colors and fonts matter and convey different messages

Keep these characteristics in mind when you select a logo for your business. I would advise against using clip art or stock images because those may not convey the image you want for the brand of your business.

Business Cards

You will want to get business cards right away so you can start handing them out. You may want the same person who creates your logo to create business cards for you as well. Alternatively, you can order business cards online from several sources; these sources often have a business card creator to help you create your own card.

Keep in mind the brand image we discussed earlier when you get business cards. You probably do not want your business cards to convey cheap or unprofessional. So, do not print them yourself on card stock from the office supply store. Do not order the free cards from Vistaprint (they have "Vistaprint" printed on the backs). You can order hundreds of quality business cards for less than $50 with a little bit of research. Remember that you want the cards to portray the right image for your company brand.

I have ordered my cards from www.overnightprints.com for many years because I like the quality of the cards. The card stock is thicker than that of most business cards and really conveys an impression of quality cards but at a reasonable price. I pay extra for rounded corners to add to the quality impression, and this differentiates my card from others.

You can order business cards online from other sources; most office supply stores offer them as well. Watch for sales and sign up for their newsletters. Stores often send out discount codes. But do not be chintzy when ordering or handing out your business cards. They are not very expensive, and you should pass out business cards freely. You may want to give people several so they can keep one and pass the others to possible referrals for you. Leave cards at businesses you frequent and distribute them in many local places such as coffee shops.

05 Set Up Your Home Office

Setting up your home office is important for many reasons. Having a dedicated place for your office helps the business to feel more professional. You want an office to help you work comfortably and efficiently. It is important to find a place in your home where you feel comfortable. Otherwise, you will not want to work in it very much. Setting up your office helps to define your work space and keep it separate in feel and purpose from your personal space.

Before you start setting up your home office, consider the following: What are your actual needs? What materials and equipment must you have to do the work efficiently and effectively? What items, although nice, may not be necessary? This issue is especially important if you are on a budget. On a budget you get the necessities first and get the other items later as you start earning some money. You may even be able to use some furniture or fixtures that you already have in your home. It is also easy to find used office furniture and fixtures, which can save you a lot of money compared with buying new.

Define the Work Space

One of the first things you should do is define the work space for your business. It is fun and exciting to set up your home office. Having an office helps many people feel they really are in business.

When defining your work space, you should consider whether you will have clients come to your home office, or if you will always go to their business or meet them in a public place. Many people do not like to have clients come to their home. With accounting and bookkeeping services, clients really have no need to go to a home office. Either you can go to the client's office or meet in a local coffee shop or other public place, whichever is more comfortable to you.

A Home Office Environment

When my husband and I built our house twenty-four years ago, we chose plans with a downstairs bedroom. We altered that room into the home office and installed many outlets on two main walls, anticipating the need for computers, printers, scanners, my assistant who comes every few months, etc. We eliminated the bedroom closet to allow for more wall room. Instead of the closet, I had bookcases installed. Two large desks run almost the length of two walls. Last year I purchased three 23-inch monitors for my computers. In one corner is my golden retriever Lexie's crate without the door. She comes in and out all day, hangs out when she wants. For additional storage, I have made use of the top of the crate by placing my big HP multifunction two-tray printer on top of it. There is also a small TV in the room and, of course, a stereo for music, which is on nonstop.

Joan Miceli-Muhlbauer, Computer Ledger Systems, www.computerledgersystems.com, Hopewell Junction, NY

In addition, take the time to consider your personal work style and preferences. You are the boss, and you can create the environment that helps you to do your best work. Some people prefer quiet, whereas others like background noise with a TV or radio on. Consider your ideal work environment when setting up your home office.

Take a tour around your home and consider where you can set up your home office. Is a spare bedroom, dining room, part of the basement, or corner of the bedroom available for your office? Consider the space that you'll need for your equipment, the traffic through that room (whether busy or not), and the logistics of the furniture setup when considering the location of the office. Where do you have room for a desk, copier, and perhaps some shelves? Look for a place that has adequate lighting—preferably a space with some windows for natural light. However, you do not want to position your desk right in front of a window due to the glare on your monitor. Find a place that will be quiet when you need to be on a business call or need to discuss confidential client information. Do you want or need a room with a door? If you have little kids, does the door lock?

The good news is that providing accounting and bookkeeping services does not require a lot of space. Plus, with electronic storage of documents, you do not even

Different Offices over the Years

Over the years I have had a couple of different home offices. In addition, the use of the Internet and sometimes remote access allows me to work from the lake, on ski trips, and on other family vacations, too. One thing I have learned about myself is that I really do not like having my office in the basement even though it is finished and nice. It tends to be colder and away from the main part of the house. For the most part, I do not like total quiet when I am working. I like having the TV or radio on in another room for some background noise.

My current office is my favorite, and I enjoy working in it. It is on the main floor of our house, painted in my favorite color (blue), and decorated to my tastes. I no longer work at the kitchen table which I often did in the past. When I need total quiet for a conference call or webinar that I am presenting, then I go to my other office downstairs, which has more storage and file cabinets. Although it had the right accessories, the downstairs office did not provide me with as much comfort as my current location. Remember that if you are not comfortable in your office, then you will not work in it as much and therefore won't be as productive in general.

need as many file cabinets as in the past. A checklist on pp. 88–89 can help you set up your office.

Furniture and Fixtures

Desk

The most obvious piece of furniture that you will need is a desk. Having a desk with adequate work space and room for two (or more) monitors, depending, of course, on your specific needs, is nice. When choosing a desk, you can spend hundreds (or thousands) of dollars, but that is not really necessary. You can find inexpensive desks at Target, Walmart, or office supply stores or used desks at garage sales, thrift stores, or on Craigslist. You can even use a couple of file cabinets and a door (or another large piece of wood) to make your own desk. If you are on a budget, do not spend a lot of money on your desk in the beginning; you can always get a nicer desk later.

Personal Touches for Your Home Office

Create a working space that will conveniently meet your needs. It has taken me about three years to get the office like I want it. I added a fax, a second monitor, and a bookcase, all things that make it easier to work and communicate and allow me to do tasks faster. It also made a big difference when I painted the room a nice color and added some plants and pictures that I liked. Personal touches like this helped because I spend a lot of time in the room. I would suggest you make sure your equipment is up to the task that you require of it. For example, I purchased a fax that can also scan, but I did not realize that it would not hook up to my computer or scan electronically. Be sure the equipment you buy serves all of your needs.

Carolyn Hunter, Cascade Accounting,
www.cascadeaccounting.net, North Bend, WA

Chair

A good office chair is important and is one of the items that you should splurge on. If you work many hours a day, you need a comfortable chair. Otherwise, you may suffer from pain in your back, shoulders, arms, and more. Ergonomics is important if you sit at a desk for hours working on the computer. You want a chair with adequate back support, adjustable height, and more. A quick Google search will help you learn more about ergonomics and how to pick out a chair and set up your desk and computer to minimize strain on your body.

When you start looking for chairs, you will find that the really good ones are fairly expensive (between $300 and $1,000). When you are just starting out, you may find spending that much money on a chair difficult. If your chair does not provide adequate back support, you can buy a back support from office supply stores for around $50, or you may find a pillow to help support your lower back.

You probably will want a chair mat, too. A chair mat can help protect your hardwood floor from scratches or enable you to move and roll easily on carpet. You can get a chair mat at office supply stores for as low as $25; however, an inexpensive one may crack within a year or so, especially if you are using the mat on carpet. You may opt for a chair mat that is a little thicker for $50–$60 instead. Many office

Home Office Is the Only Option

With the family room being a good-sized room, I was able to set up my home office in one of the corners of this room. The L-shaped desk fits perfectly and gives me plenty of room to work. The file cabinet is next to the desk, very convenient.

Because I am legally blind and live out in the country, working out of the home was the only way I could have my own business. I don't have to rely on anybody to get me to work. Plus, I am saving my precious time by not having to travel from one client to another. That time saved allows me to be more available to spend time with my husband, my kids, and my dogs. I can still keep up with all the household chores and get dinner on the table when the family comes home.

Laura Kaniuk, LJK Bookkeeping Services,
www.ljkbooks.com, DeMotte, IN

supply stores have coupons regularly, so look for one in the paper or online prior to your purchase.

Lighting

Your home office should have adequate lighting. Natural light from windows is preferable; however, you do not want to place your desk right in front of the window due to the glare from the light on your monitor. You will need some lamps to provide additional lighting as well. Consider getting both floor lamps and task lighting for your desk.

File Cabinets

In the past you needed a lot of filing cabinets for all the client records and files. Now, with the ability to scan and store documents electronically, you need fewer filing cabinets. However, you still probably will need some space to store files. Your desk may provide a couple of drawers for files that you use most frequently. Store files you use only periodically in a file cabinet in another room or closet if there is insufficient space in your office. For efficiency purposes, you should keep the files you use frequently nearby in your office. Used filing cabinets can often be found to save money, or you can use file boxes for storage.

Storage Space and Shelves

You may need storage space for office supplies as well. You may use storage cabinets or shelves. Some people use old kitchen cabinets (painted or not), dressers, or shelves with baskets to store copier paper, ink or toner, or other office supplies. You may want shelves to hold textbooks or other references. If you are on a budget, you can get creative to find storage space and shelves. How the shelving looks is less important than how functional the shelving is. Remember that you need to be organized but that your clients probably will not see your storage space.

Other Miscellaneous Items

You might need several other miscellaneous items in your home office. These include:

- Trash can and a shredder for confidential information
- Fan or space heater, depending on the HVAC setup in your home office
- Clock
- Decorations, pictures, plants, and other decor
- Whiteboard, calendar, or bulletin board

Technology: Computer, Software, and Other Equipment

For providing accounting and bookkeeping services, a computer is not only essential but also the most important thing for your business. You may already have a computer that you can use; however, it needs to be no older than a couple of years to run the current software adequately. If you will purchase a new computer, you should consider several factors, which we will discuss in detail below.

P.C. or Mac?

When buying a computer, the first thing to decide is whether to get a P.C. with Windows software or a Mac. Mac computers have been increasing in popularity because they can now run Windows programs. However, in order for them to run Windows programs, you need to purchase a software adapter, and it may not operate without some problems. I recommend using a P.C. because the vast majority of business clients will use P.C.s and most accounting software requires Windows software.

Thoughts from a Home-Based CPA

Tell us about your home office

For nearly six years I had my office in the living room of our house, which was close to the front door. I could see out the front window, see when the mail came, and see when a client would drive up. A lot of light came in through the windows. I had my own room air conditioner to keep me cool. The office was cramped, however, and I had little privacy. We set it up that way originally because it was the only space we had available in the home. And, if clients came to see me, they would not have to go far into the house.

In addition, my wife has a weak immune system. For her health we realized (as an afterthought) we shouldn't let people into the house at all to prevent the risk that they drag in sickness and germs and therefore make our house unsafe. I distinctly remember when a sick client came through the home and exposed my family to her cold.

As a result, I started meeting people at a nearby restaurant, which is very close to my house and easy for clients to find. The restaurant was always clean, fairly quiet, and inexpensive, and no waiter or waitress made you feel guilty for taking up one of their tables for an hour or two. One year I calculated that I was there between seventy to eighty times for meetings. The management didn't mind (as long as I didn't come in during their rush hour time), and they loved all the business I brought them.

This tax season my home office was moved to the family room at garden level in the back of the house. There is no more front window and no more room air conditioner, but I do have the swamp cooler, and the room's temperature is a little cooler at garden level. There is also a lot more room for me, my desks, and all my stuff. I set up an aluminum camp table and use it when I need more work surface. I even have a twin-size air mattress down here for naps when I need them.

Ironically, I moved down here so that my wife could have her living room back; she often said she was tired of it being an office. Now guess who set up her office, with desk, file cabinets, bookshelves, etc., right where my office was? Yes, you guessed it: my wife, who is studying for her master's in counseling. And, go figure, she has my room air conditioner now.

What is the best thing about working from home?

I like the low overhead and that I can work crazy hours when I need to. When I worked for a CPA firm with an office, and the kids were younger, my wife would call at about 9 o'clock and ask if I was coming home soon. That ended the late nights then and there. Plus, office buildings get spooky that late at night. Now I can be here working and still be a part of my family. If the kids need a ride somewhere, I can help out (sometimes). I can still see what is going on in their lives and be around to participate (sometimes too much). One night I just couldn't sleep so I got up at one in the morning and worked until 5 a.m. It was nice and quiet, and I was very productive. Try that in a regular office setting. And, like others will say, you don't have to dress up all the time. T-shirts and shorts are regular summer working gear.

What do you not like about working from home?

Lack of real privacy is a big one. My wife sometimes hears my phone conversations (she is only 15 feet away or so on the next level up). And it gets really noisy here sometimes. The other day I was on the phone with a client, and my wife and oldest child got into a fight with lots of yelling at each other. My client didn't need to hear that kind of stuff, so I went into the bathroom and closed the door to keep the sound down. I also started password locking my computers to be proactive against someone possibly breaking into my house and stealing the computers with all the client data on them. But I also found out that my family likes to snoop and use my computers when I am not around. They have their own computers, so there is no need to be on my work ones.

There is also a general sense that because I work from home, I don't actually work. For example, sometimes my wife thinks that, because I work at home, I can just drop what I am doing to run errands to her (things she forgot, doctor appointments, grocery runs, etc.). There are times I can do these things and I don't mind, but sometimes they come at really bad times. I have on occasion had to say no, I have a conflict.

There are times I wish I had a real office again, but I would feel obligated to keep office hours, and I know I would be dragging work home anyway. So why not save $1,000 a month or more by working at home?

Do you have any advice or suggestions for others wanting to start working from home?

One thing I wish I had done differently was to get a brand new phone number for my office rather than convert the family phone number to business. I didn't have the choice when I went out on my own. Unfortunately it meant that I sometimes got family calls on my business line. By getting an entirely new phone line dedicated strictly to business, you won't have that conflict.

One other thing I did that has really worked for us is to purchase the message notification service from our telephone company. It's an extra feature for about $6 a month. When someone leaves a message on my home/office phone, the message notification service calls my cell phone almost immediately and lets me hear the message. This is not the same as call forwarding. I don't want all my calls forwarded to my cell phone. This service tells me when I have a voice mail so I don't have to keep checking it all the time, and if a client calls and leaves a message, I get the message right away and can respond to it or not. I also got a private mailbox at the UPS store with a real street address on it. I use that for client mail that used to come to my house. It's pretty handy to have a place for clients to send mail to other than my house.

Mark E. Edgar, CPA PC, Aurora, CO

Desktop or Laptop?

In the past desktop computers were much more powerful than notebooks or laptops (these terms will be used interchangeably). However, that situation has changed as notebook computers have debuted in the marketplace with faster processing chips, more RAM, and much more affordable prices. I switched to a notebook computer many years ago and have not had a desktop computer in a long time. I like the portability and flexibility of a notebook computer because it allows me to work anywhere. With wireless Internet and a notebook computer, you can work anywhere inside your house or even outside (within reason, depending on your wireless connection capabilities). When you travel, you can take it with you and work as needed.

Along with the notebook computer, you may want to get a full-size keyboard and mouse. These allow you to work comfortably at your desk with the portability of a notebook. Often you can buy a wireless keyboard and mouse together for around

$50 at office supply stores. You may opt for an ergonomic keyboard, which may cost a little more. But if it is more comfortable for you to work on, then the money may be well spent.

If you are using a notebook or laptop computer, then you may want to get a universal port replicator (i.e., docking station) to expand the number of USB ports available. This allows you to plug in the printer, mouse, keyboard, charging cables and more.

Apple's iPad computer has generated a lot of interest for tablet computers. As a result, more companies are entering the market to offer this style of computer. Tablet computers are based on various operating systems (like the Mac, Droid, or others). Before purchasing a tablet computer you should research whether your programs will operate on the tablet or not. For example, QuickBooks Pro currently cannot be installed on an iPad. Companies are creating new apps and things are changing quickly in this area. Research the latest information to make an informed purchase.

Computer: Processor Speed, RAM, and Hard Drive

I cannot give specific recommendations on computer specifications because these recommendations most likely will be outdated within a few months since technology gets better and faster all the time. However, it is possible to discuss general guidelines to help you when selecting a computer.

If you are buying a new computer, look for one with a fast processor, fast enough to run accounting software (such as QuickBooks or Peachtree) and Microsoft Office. You don't need to buy the top-of-the-line, most expensive computer in the store. The most important consideration is to have a computer with enough RAM (random access memory), which is not very expensive (and you can usually add more RAM at a later time if needed). The amount of RAM you have can directly affect the speed of your computer.

When it comes to the hard drive, you can buy an external hard drive later if needed. Most people would recommend you back up your hard drive files on an external hard drive for safekeeping. You can find an adequate notebook (or desktop) computer starting at about $500. Because the prices are more reasonable now due to increasing options in the marketplace (versus $2,000 starting costs years ago), I have started buying a new computer every two to three years. I am not a techie, so updating often prevents problems with hard drives crashing and keeps me current with technology and operating systems.

Monitors

I suggest you get another monitor so you have dual monitors (or a really large monitor). After you start working with two monitors, you will wonder how you ever worked with just one. You can have your e-mail open on one monitor while working in a client data file on the other screen. Or you can have a client bank statement (or other document) open on one screen while you are reconciling or entering data on the other monitor. Having dual monitors open improves your efficiency (particularly with electronic documents, such as PDFs) and eliminates the need to print documents (saving you money as well). Some people use even three or four monitors now. With Windows 7 (and Vista) operating systems, it is easy to plug in a second monitor to extend your desktop.

Backups

I was surprised to learn that hard drives in computers do not have a very long life expectancy (three to five years). This limitation is why IT people usually say that it is not a question of *if* your hard drive will fail but rather a question of *when* it will fail. This is why you should have some kind of a reliable backup system in place. Numerous online backup services (Mozy, Carbonite, etc.) are automatic and ensure you have an off-site backup. I recommend that people also back up locally to an external hard drive or even to a USB flash drive to ensure they have duplicate backups.

You should test your backup system to ensure that it is working properly and that the backup can be restored. I had a client who assured me that the data was safe and that the network backup every night was sufficient. However, it had never been tested. When the system failed, the client was unable to restore the backup. The client was a multimillion-dollar contractor with a lot of financial transactions. The client finally found a backup of the QuickBooks data file, but this backup was about four months old. This tale demonstrates the importance of testing the backup system and having even duplicate backup procedures. Backing up a QuickBooks file to an external hard drive or USB drive periodically is not difficult. (Note: Always backup QuickBooks to the hard drive and then copy the file to an external hard drive or USB drive. Do not try to go directly to external drives.)

Printer/Copier

When it comes to printers, you have lots of options. Laser or inkjet? Color or black and white? Take some time to think about your needs for the services you provide.

With the ability to create and send PDFs, many accounting professionals find that they do not print nearly as much as in the past.

When considering whether to get a laser or inkjet printer, keep in mind that laser printers are generally faster and cost less per page to print. The ink cartridges are fairly costly, but many people purchase refilled ink cartridges or a refill kit to do it themselves. These refillable ink cartridges appear to work fine for many people and save money on ink, too.

Do you need to print in color? If you will need to print reports with charts and graphs for clients, then you may want a color printer. Otherwise, it may not be necessary.

Should you purchase a multifunction printer, scanner, copier, or individual components? It depends on your needs. If you are just getting started, then a multifunction printer will probably work fine for you. However, if you are scanning lots of documents, then you may prefer a more robust scanner than the one in a multifunction printer.

When you are shopping for a printer, remember to look for pages per minute to help compare printers. Also, do not buy features that you do not want and will probably never use—why pay more?

Scanner

More and more people are trying to go paperless and are scanning documents to store them electronically (i.e., on the computer, an external hard drive, or online storage service). Many scanners are available, but you should make sure to get one that is TWAIN compliant. (TWAIN is an industry standard scanner driver that allows you to seamlessly connect your scanner to hundreds of scanning applications.)

Just as with printers, you should consider several options when selecting a scanner. Do you need a flatbed scanner—will you need to scan from books or magazines? Most accounting professionals prefer a sheet-fed scanner.

Do you want a scanner with duplex scanning (i.e., it scans both sides of the paper)? If you will scan mostly text, you do not need high resolution. Also, consider if you want one for your desktop or if you want a portable one, which would be convenient to take on-site to clients' offices. Keep in mind that you will probably need to feed each document separately with a portable scanner. Desktop scanners have sheet-feeders where you can insert several pages to scan without feeding them through one at a time.

Some scanners come with Adobe Acrobat Pro to help you work with PDFs, and some are bundled with scanning software such as Rack2-Filer. Scanning software helps you organize and manage the documents you have stored electronically.

Fax

With the ability to scan and e-mail documents, many people no longer use a fax machine. I personally have not used a fax in many years. You can use online e-fax services if you need to fax something. Or you can always go to a nearby office supply store or elsewhere to fax. Unless you have a real need to fax documents frequently, then I would suggest you not purchase a fax machine.

Phone

You should have a dedicated phone line for your business. You do not want your kids, spouse, or significant other answering a business call. However, more and more people are using their cell phones exclusively for business, and some use different ring tones to help identify callers.

You may want to get a headset to allow you to talk hands-free. This arrangement can be beneficial when talking with clients, working remotely with clients, or taking part in conference calls or webinars. Headsets are inexpensive and can be purchased at office supply stores, Walmart, or Target. You need to make sure your phone has a jack to plug in the headset. If you have a Bluetooth phone, then you may prefer to get a wireless headset.

When it comes to using phones and talking with people, consider these developments:

- Google Talk is an application that you can download to your computer. You can text chat and send files to people. You can also call (computer to computer) people for free—anywhere in the world.
- According to Google, Inc., its Google Voice app provides one phone number for all of your phones, free long-distance calling throughout the United States, and voice mail that's as easy to use as e-mail.
- Skype allows you to make Internet calls for free to others who use Skype, and you can do video calls and screen sharing, too. Paid plans with more features are also available.

Internet and Online Services

You will need an Internet service that is fast and reliable. Fast and reliable service is especially important if you will provide remote consulting or training. I recommend you set up wireless Internet so you can work anywhere in your home or outside, too. Setting up a wireless network in your home is easier than ever, and wireless routers are not very expensive either (between $50–$100). You can get wireless printers, too.

If you will travel or if your area does not have high-speed Internet service, then you may consider getting broadband service from your cell phone provider. All the major wireless phone providers (Verizon, AT&T, Sprint, etc.) provide an option for broadband for your computer. If you need only occasional use, then you may consider tethering your cell phone to your computer for occasional use as well. Check out software such as Tether or contact your cell phone company for details.

Accounting Software

Obviously if you will provide accounting and bookkeeping services, then you will need an accounting program. The first question is whether to use QuickBooks or Peachtree. When I started my business (about twenty years ago), I purchased Peachtree Complete Accounting and used it for many years. However, I found that more and more clients were using QuickBooks, so I started using it as well. Eventually I quit using Peachtree and used QuickBooks exclusively for about the past fifteen years or more. I found trying to stay current on both programs difficult. QuickBooks has roughly 90 percent market share, and the vast majority of small businesses use QuickBooks. However, Peachtree is preferable when dealing with more complex inventory such as First-in, first-out (FIFO) or Last-in, last-out (LIFO) which is not available in Quickbooks. It is important to consider the needs of your clients. If you have larger clients with more complex accounting needs, then you may need to consider programs other than QuickBooks or they may need QuickBooks combined with an industry-specific application to meet the client's needs. There are thousands of third-party programs available. Check out http://marketplace.intuit.com.

Several versions of QuickBooks are available—QuickBooks Pro, QuickBooks Premier, QuickBooks Accountant, QuickBooks Enterprise, and various editions of QuickBooks Online. You could purchase QuickBooks Pro and perform monthly bookkeeping for clients. However, I recommend QuickBooks Accountant Edition, which includes several unique features for accounting professionals (that are not available in QuickBooks Pro), such as:

- Accountant's Copy: You can convert an Accountant's Copy file and export changes for clients to import into their QuickBooks file. (Read the QuickBooks help menu for details about working with an Accountant's Copy and what does or does not go back and other details.)
- Client Data Review: This enables you to find and fix numerous problems in clients' QuickBooks data files.
- Intuit Statement Writer (sold separately): This allows you to customize clients' financial statements and reports with a live link to the QuickBooks data so it automatically updates when you enter changes in the QuickBooks data file.
- Working Trial Balance: This provides the beginning balance, client activity, adjusting entries, and the ending balance and includes a place for work paper references or notes.
- Fixed Asset Manager: This allows you to manage and calculate depreciation on fixed assets and integrates with QuickBooks.
- Adjust and Reversing Journal Entries
- Toggle: You can toggle into other editions of QuickBooks (for the same year) to see the same screen as the client (QuickBooks Pro and QuickBooks Premier Editions).

Rather than just purchasing the QuickBooks Accountant program, I suggest you join the ProAdvisor Program, which includes the program and numerous other benefits as discussed in the next section.

QuickBooks ProAdvisor Program

If you will provide accounting and bookkeeping services to clients, then I recommend joining the QuickBooks ProAdvisor Program. Joining the program currently costs $499, and provides many benefits, including:

- Programs and software:
    QuickBooks Accountant
    QuickBooks Enterprise Solutions–Accountant Edition (single user)
    QuickBooks Online (subscription for the year of your membership)
- Dedicated U.S.-based technical support (during normal business hours and offshore after hours and holidays)
- Certification courses and exams: You can get certified in QuickBooks, QuickBooks Enterprise Solutions, and QuickBooks Point of Sale—all are optional

and included with the membership fee (i.e., the certification courses and exams have no additional cost). The certification is discussed in depth in the next chapter.

- Your profile listed on the Find a ProAdvisor website after you are certified in QuickBooks: This referral website gets an average of forty thousand hits per month and is a great source for potential clients to find you. After you pass the QuickBooks Certified ProAdvisor exam, you will be listed for free, and the listings are optimized to be included in Google (and other) search results.
- Optional (additional fee of $175): QuickBooks Enhanced Payroll for Accountants, which will allow you to process payroll for up to fifty clients (EINs)
- Other discounts and benefits (details at http://proadvisor.intuit.com)

Overall I think the ProAdvisor program is a great value, and I recommend joining it. You renew membership each year which allows you to get the new software every year as well. Having numerous years of QuickBooks helps you to meet the needs of your clients because QuickBooks is not backward compatible. Plus, QuickBooks Pro or QuickBooks Accountant cannot open files from QuickBooks Enterprise Solutions.

Bottom Line: Ask Questions

Do you have any advice or suggestions for others wanting to start working from home?
Have your business cards ready and hand them out everywhere you go. Create a website using specific keywords of your business; give discounts or advertise specials. It will take some time to establish a client base and momentum, so don't be hard on yourself if you don't see immediate results. It's important to keep trying and market yourself. QuickBooks is a good accounting program to use, and becoming a Certified QuickBooks ProAdvisor does have its advantages. If you're not able to get into the QuickBooks program right now, make it a part of your business plan to invest in down the road. I did this when I first started; I purchased the ProAdvisor Program with Enhanced Payroll for Accountants and studied the course materials to pass the exams for each year that the exam came out. And most importantly, ask questions—don't ever be afraid to ask questions!
Sheryl Theis, SET the Mark Bookkeeping-Payroll-Taxes-Notary Public, www.taxesbookkeeping.net, Humble, TX

With the ProAdvisor Program, you get a single-user copy of QuickBooks Enterprise Solutions–Accountant Edition so you can support those clients, too.

Microsoft Office

As a small business owner, you will most likely need Word, Excel, Outlook, and PowerPoint programs. Alternatives exist; however, Office programs integrate with QuickBooks, and many of your clients will use them as well. You may use Excel frequently when calculating budgets or forecasts, creating charts, graphs, and pivot tables, or other uses.

When Microsoft Office 2010 was released, Microsoft also released Office 2010 suite online for free. It may be worth exploring to see if it would meet your needs.

If you purchase the desktop version of Microsoft Office 2010, be aware that many programs do not work with the 64-bit version of it. It is recommended to install the 32-bit version of Office 2010 instead.

Antivirus, Firewall, Security

You definitely need to protect your computer. Numerous options are available—some free programs do a pretty good job, too. Some frequently mentioned programs are AVG and Avast (both have free and paid versions) and Trend Micro (which does not have a free version). However, as with all technology and software, these programs can change frequently. I would suggest you do a Google search for reviews and comments (from *PC World*, among others) or ask IT specialists, Geek Squad employees, or others for their recommendations.

Even more important is to ensure that you are careful not to click on any links in e-mails or social media. Often the e-mails can look like the real thing from a bank, the IRS, Intuit, or others. Rather than click on a link in an e-mail, go to the website. Also, when you use social media such as Facebook, be careful about clicking links there as well. I suggest you utilize the free Web of Trust tool (www.mywot.com) which helps ensure you do not visit "bad" websites. It is free, easy to use, and effective to help you identify trustworthy and safe websites.

If you suspect that your computer has a virus, do not immediately back up your computer because you will back up the virus as well. Many times you can perform a system restore (through Windows), which will restore your system to a point prior to when the computer was infected. Doing this is often the fastest and most efficient method to remove a virus. However, some viruses wipe out all of your system restore points. In this situation try starting your computer in safe mode (press F8 before the Windows logo appears to select to start in safe mode) and running your antivirus program to scan and remove the virus. You may need to use more than one antivirus program because sometimes one program will find the virus when another one missed it. If you are unable to fix the computer yourself, then you may need to take the computer in to get help. The best course is to try to prevent viruses in the first place by using antivirus software or Web of Trust as mentioned previously (www.myweb.com). Remember to be careful of the links you click, the websites you browse, and what you download.

Adobe Acrobat—PDFs

A PDF printer is a great way to save documents as PDF files. For example, if you make an online purchase you can print your receipt or confirmation to PDF format and save it electronically instead of printing it on paper. You can get free PDF printers from www.cutePDF.com or www.bullzip.com.

Even more powerful is Adobe Acrobat (not the free Adobe Reader). With Adobe Acrobat you can not only print to PDF format but also use the program as a typewriter to fill in PDF forms or sign PDFs electronically with your digital signature. For example, if someone sends you a document to sign, you can use Adobe Acrobat to sign it electronically instead of printing it out, signing it, and scanning it to return to sender. Passwords and other security features protect your electronic signature as well.

Office Supplies

You will need some basic office supplies to get your business up and running; a great time to buy them is during the back-to-school sales in the summer and winter. Some things you may need include:

- Copier paper
- Ink or toner cartridge
- Stapler, staples, and staple remover
- Paper or binder clips
- Note pads or writing paper
- Folders and labels
- Report binding machine, covers, and related supplies, if you provide hardcopy reports for clients

Checklist for Setting up Your Home Office

	Estimated Cost	Completed	Notes
Define Your Space			
Furniture and Fixtures			
Desk			
Chair			
Chair mat			
Lighting			
Natural light			
Overhead			
Task lamps			
File cabinet			
Shelves			
Storage space			
Trash can			
Shredder			
Space heater or fan			
Clock			
Decorations			
Plants			
Pictures			
Other decor			
White board, calendar, or bulletin board			
Technology			
Computer			
Monitors (dual preferably)			

	Estimated Cost	Completed	Notes
Backups			
External hard drive			
Online backup service			
Printer/copier			
Fax			
Phone			
Internet/wireless			
Accounting software			
Payroll software			
Tax software			
Microsoft Office or alternative			
Antivirus/security			
Adobe Acrobat (optional)			
Office Supplies			
Copier paper			
Ink or toner			
Stapler, staples, and remover			
Paper clips or binder clips			
Note pads or writing paper			
Folders and labels			
Report binding machine and supplies (optional)			
Pens, pencils, erasers			
Calculator			

- Pens, pencils, erasers, etc.
- Calculator—or use MoffSoft (www.moffsoft.com) free calculator on your computer. It is better than the built-in Windows calculator, and many accounting professionals use it.

Resist the urge to buy office supplies you may not actually need. With so much being done online and electronically now, you do not need as many office supplies as in the past.

06 Training, Certification, and Experience

The type of training or certification you need will vary based on your education, experience, and other certifications. Below are suggestions that may or may not apply to your specific situation.

Bookkeeping or Accounting

If you are going to provide bookkeeping and accounting services, then you should have some education or training in bookkeeping. Several ways to get this education exist, and you should evaluate each one to determine which is right to meet your needs and budget.

Community College

Many community colleges offer accounting or bookkeeping classes, and the tuition is reasonable for nearby residents. You should contact the school to find out if it will allow you to enroll in these classes as a non-degree seeking student (unless you want to pursue a degree or more).

The benefit of taking a class at a local community college is the instructor is available to ask questions of in person and to help ensure you understand the material. In addition, if you get to know the instructors, then they may be future references, resources, or possibly even mentors as you start and grow your business.

Penn Foster

Penn Foster (www.pennfoster.edu) is an online "career school" that provides bookkeeping training from the comfort and convenience of your home. According to the school's website, the school allows you to "earn your Bookkeeping Career Diploma from Regionally and Nationally Accredited Penn Foster Career

School. Over 13 million students have enrolled in our training programs, making Penn Foster one of the world's largest and most respected distance learning institutions." I have heard others speak highly of their training from Penn Foster, and it is not too costly. It was around $700, which included the textbooks and materials, but Penn Foster was offering a $100 discount, making the cost around $600.

In addition, Penn Foster includes materials to help you prepare for the American Institute of Professional Bookkeepers (AIPB) certification and "a voucher to defray the cost of your AIPB exam."

Other Online Courses, Training, or Cerifications

Numerous online programs, schools, training centers, organizations, etc. offer accounting or bookkeeping courses, training, or certifications. Many of these can be quite costly, and unfortunately some of them are not reputable. I would suggest you do some research before signing up with an online program or organization. Google the company or organization name (search using abbreviations and spelled out completely) along with various terms, such as *complaints*, *comments*, *reviews*, *scams*, etc., to evaluate whether the program is the right choice for you. You can also join bookkeeping or accounting groups or forums online and ask for comments or experiences from other people to help you make an informed decision. Do not rely purely on claims from the program's website or the admissions officer or whomever you might talk to on the phone. If you are going to spend $1,500 or more, which is to be expected for some online training programs such as these, then you should be cautious prior to purchase. Do your due diligence on online training programs or certifications from organizations.

Bookkeeper Certification

Earning certifications can enhance your credibility with clients. In addition, it can help differentiate you from other bookkeepers. Based on the 2010 Certified Bookkeeper Survey from the American Institute of Professional Bookkeepers (discussed below), the Certified Bookkeepers who responded reported numerous benefits to certification, including the following:

- Increased self-confidence
- Filled in gaps in knowledge
- Gained knowledge

- Increased professional pride
- Enhanced self-image
- Enhanced standing with employer or clients

In addition, about one-third of them reported increasing the rates they charged to clients after earning the certification. Clearly getting certified can be beneficial for numerous reasons. If you decide to become a Certified Bookkeeper, you can consider several certifications.

American Institute of Professional Bookkeepers

The American Institute of Professional Bookkeepers offers the Certified Bookkeeper designation (CB). The AIPB (www.aipb.org) has been around since 1987 and its mission statement is the following:

"The American Institute of Professional Bookkeepers is the bookkeeping profession's national association. AIPB's mission is to achieve recognition of bookkeepers as accounting professionals; keep bookkeepers up to date on changes in bookkeeping, accounting and tax; answer bookkeepers' everyday bookkeeping and accounting questions; and certify bookkeepers who meet high, national standards."

To become a Certified Bookkeeper, you must have two years of full-time experience (or the part time equivalent), sign a code of ethics, and pass a four-part national exam as follows:

1. Adjusting entries and error correction
2. Payroll and depreciation
3. Inventory
4. Internal controls and fraud prevention

The first two exams are proctored exams at a Prometric test center (centers are located nationwide with a testing fee of about $100). The last two exams are open-workbook tests you can complete at home and send in for grading. In addition, after you are certified, you must obtain continuing education every three years to maintain certification. Full details are available at www.aipb.org. The Certified Bookkeeper designation is the only one mentioned by the U.S. Department of Labor in the Bureau of Labor Statistics. The proctored exams and experience requirement make the CB somewhat more difficult to obtain, but those requirements also help to distinguish this certification. You can earn the experience requirement after taking the exams. You can request a twenty-three-page booklet from the AIPB for more details (see the website, www.aipb.org/certification_program.htm).

The cost to earn the Certified Bookkeeper designation is $500 to $600, depending on whether or not you are a member of AIPB. This cost assumes that you pass all four tests the first time (fees are charged for retesting). But the cost includes all the registrations, books, etc.

Universal Accounting

Universal Accounting offers the Professional Bookkeeper (PB) designation and provides training in accounting and tax services. The program from Universal Accounting (www.universalaccounting.com) includes more than just bookkeeping/accounting training. It covers topics such as marketing and growing your business, helps you create and host a website (for six months), and offers some additional practice sets. The program from Universal Accounting costs between $1,500 and $2,000 and is the most expensive of those mentioned here. Research the company online to learn more about what others have to say to help you make a decision as to which certification is right for you. Whether you sign up for the program or not, you should check out the free newsletters (in free resources) on the website. Universal Accounting has some good marketing ideas and other tips, too.

National Association of Certified Public Bookkeepers

The National Association of Certified Public Bookkeepers (NACPB) offers the designations Certified Public Bookkeeper (CPB), Certified Payroll Specialist, and Certified Quickbooks Advisor (which is *not* the same as Intuit's Certified ProAdvisor designation discussed in the next section). The NACPB states that its mission is to:

> "... protect and assure the public that members are trusted and competent by offering nationally recognized public bookkeeper certifications and licenses. Public bookkeepers use these accreditations to gain a competitive edge by distinguishing themselves from other public bookkeepers."

The CPB exam is a three-part exam that is taken online from your home or wherever you prefer. It covers accounting, payroll, and financial management. It is an open-book exam, and you can take each part separately. After you start one part of the exam, you have twenty-four hours to complete that part of the exam.

QuickBooks Certified ProAdvisor

In the previous chapter I recommended joining the QuickBooks ProAdvisor program (http://proadvisor.intuit.com). The ProAdvisor membership includes access to the certification courses and exams at no additional cost. You can earn several certifications, starting with QuickBooks Certified ProAdvisor, which requires you to pass an online exam. Nine training courses help you prepare for the certification exam:

- Course 1: Product Overview—How to Choose, Recommend, and Stay Up to Date
- Course 2: Setting Up QuickBooks
- Course 3: Recording Transactions in QuickBooks
- Course 4: Reporting in QuickBooks
- Course 5: Year-end Procedures and Periodic Tasks
- Course 6: Setting Up and Using Payroll, Including Time Tracking
- Course 7: Importing and Exporting Data from QuickBooks
- Course 8: Special Considerations and Troubleshooting
- Course 9: What Is New for 2011

After you pass the exam and are certified, you will be listed on the Find a ProAdvisor website. As previously mentioned, this referral database gets an average of forty thousand hits per month. Potential clients can search by zip code, specialization, or other criteria. Completing your profile to help potential clients find you is important.

In addition to the Certified ProAdvisor designation, you can get certified in QuickBooks Enterprise Solutions and/or QuickBooks Point of Sale. Both are included with your ProAdvisor membership. Training courses can help you learn more about these programs and earn the certification. The additional certifications can help you further differentiate yourself and attract other potential clients.

If you decide to pursue the additional certifications, I would recommend you work on the certification for QuickBooks Enterprise Solutions (QBES) first. QBES is similar to QuickBooks with the same look and feel but has more features and a more powerful, underlying database. But with the training materials available, learning more about it and earning the QBES certification does not require a significant amount of time.

However, QuickBooks Point of Sale is a totally separate program. Training materials and resources are available for it; however, earning that certification will probably take you longer than the QBES certification.

Other Certifications

In addition to getting certified as a bookkeeper or for QuickBooks, you may decide to earn other certifications. Depending on your interests and the services you plan to offer, some of the other most common certifications include the following:

- Payroll: The American Payroll Association (APA) offers the Certified Payroll Professional (CPP) certification for those with payroll knowledge and experience or the Fundamental Payroll Certification (FPC) for payroll beginners and service and support professionals with payroll knowledge. No experience is required for the FPC, and it may be one you would want to work on first. Details can be found at www.americanpayroll.org/certification.
- Accounting: Several certifications and designations exist:
    Certified Public Accountant (CPA)—in general requires taking 150 college hours (five years of college), passing a rigorous four-part, online exam (proctored), and having two years of experience working under a CPA. The requirements vary by state; but this certification is difficult to obtain. Details at www.aicpa.org.
    Various other accounting designations, including:
    - Certified Managerial Accountant (CMA)—Details at www.imanet .org/cma-certification.aspx
    - Certified Fraud Examiner (CFE)—Details at www.acfe.com
    - Enrolled Agent (EA): This designation is earned by passing a rigorous online exam or is based upon IRS experience. Get details at the National Association of Enrolled Agents (www.naea.org).
    Other certifications and designations exist; this is a list of the just most common ones. If you are interested in additional certifications, do your research (Google is a great place to start) and ask others for their opinions and recommendations.

Experience

In addition to training and certifications, you should try to get experience before you start working with your own clients. Saying exactly how much or which type of experience would be best for you is difficult. However, you should attempt to get a variety of experiences working with companies from different industries and doing different bookkeeping tasks as well.

So where can you get experience? Perhaps you can get a bookkeeping job with a company. Another option would be to work for an accounting temporary agency to get experience working for a variety of companies. You could volunteer to help local nonprofit organizations such as homeowners' associations, churches, scouts, soccer clubs, etc.

You may want to contact other accounting professionals or Certified ProAdvisors to see if you can work for them. If you contact other accounting firms, you may be able to get a full-time job with them or simply work during their busy season. (Note: You should start contacting them in the autumn, after October 15, which is the due date for individual tax returns that were extended.) If you cannot get a job with a larger firm, try the smaller firms or sole proprietors who may really need some help but are not ready to hire a full-time staff member.

07 Marketing Your Business

An important aspect of starting and growing your home-based bookkeeping business is the need for marketing—continuously.

Your Brand

Think about what the brand will be for you and your business. Your brand is everything about you and your firm: the name, website, logo, colors, fonts, how the phone is answered, communications, e-mail signatures, your dress and appearance, and everything else, big or small. You are the business, and you must remember that when you are in public as well—you never know when you may meet an existing or potential client.

When people describe your business, what words or phrases do you want them to use? Most likely you want them to describe your business as professional, ethical, attentive to detail, and other positive characteristics. You do not want them to use negative words such as *cheap*, *sloppy*, or *careless*. Keep that in mind with everything you do. Do not print your own business cards (or get the free ones with a company name on the back). Your website should not have any misspellings, clip art (use images instead), and so on. You really must pay attention to the details on everything.

Presenting a professional image does not mean you have to be boring. Some accounting firms are getting more creative and letting their personality show. For example, one CPA firm owner has a fun personality and lets it show on his company website, in his blog, and even in his tagline, "We're not your daddy's CPA firm." The image is professional yet fun.

Your Ideal Client

The nice aspect of having your own business and being your own boss is that you can choose your clients and the services you provide. If you do not like or

> **Marketing Is Everything You Say and Everything You Do**
>
> On my business phone line I receive quite a few wrong numbers for various reasons. Yesterday I saw that I had two missed calls from the same number. There was a voice mail from a guy trying to reach someone other than me (a wrong number). This guy is an installer of something and needed to make an appointment with whoever he was trying to call. I called him and told him that he had the wrong number, blah, blah, etc. Have a great day. Five minutes later he called me back and asked about my services, informed me that although he keeps good records he has yet to file his 2009 taxes, and asked if I handle businesses. Long and short of it is that he will be in next week for me to do his taxes and then would like me to take care of his bookkeeping on a monthly basis.
>
> I can't remember where I heard it . . . but it's true. Marketing is everything you say and everything you do . . .
>
> Lori Thompson, EA, KJT Tax, www.ktjtax.com, Paw Paw, IL

enjoy working with a particular client, then you do not have to work with that person. You can "fire" clients. Doing this may be hard for you when you are just starting your business. However, keep it in mind as your business grows and you have a larger client base. Try to identify your ideal client; doing this can help you evaluate potential clients and target ones whom you would like to get as clients.

When considering who your ideal client would be, consider these questions: Would it be a small, one-person company or a small business with several employees? Would you work for the client on-site, or would he be a client with whom you could work remotely? Would he be organized and provide information timely? Would he be on time for meetings and appointments? Would he have a calm demeanor or a type-A personality? What about his ethics and business dealings?

Finding Your First Clients

Your first few clients will be the hardest to get. When you are starting your business, you need to tell anyone and everyone that you are in business and looking for clients. A former employer may be your first client or help refer you to others who need your services. A recent discussion in my LinkedIn group asked people to tell how they got their first clients. Here are a few of the answers:

- Referred by a neighbor, friend, or a CPA
- QuickBooks Find a ProAdvisor website
- Teaching QuickBooks seminars
- Member of the chamber of commerce
- Volunteering for an event
- Contractor working on my home

You can see that the first clients can come from a variety of sources, but many come from referrals or networking. You need to pass out your business cards to everyone: family, friends, neighbors, other parents of kids on Little League teams, businesses you frequent, local restaurants, or coffee shops.

When I started my business, I obtained a list of new businesses from city hall. I called them and congratulated them on starting their new business. I introduced myself, mentioned the services I provided, and said if they ever need help, please give me a call. That is how I got my first couple of clients. Plus, another client called me to do his taxes many months later! I let my first clients know that I was looking for more clients and that I would appreciate referrals. As they met with other business owners at chamber of commerce luncheons and the discussion of accounting or taxes came up, they would hand out my business card for me. Referrals are a great marketing method that we'll discuss in more detail later.

Some people have found their first few clients using Craigslist. You should be careful if you choose to use Craigslist and keep security in mind. You can monitor the postings for people looking for accounting or bookkeeping help. If you choose to post your availability on Craigslist, never provide your phone number or other confidential information. Plus, you may ask people to include a certain code word in an e-mail reply so you know it is a legitimate response as opposed to the numerous spam e-mails that you may get after posting something. The types of clients you find on Craigslist may be looking for someone cheap, and they may not be ideal clients. However, when you are starting out, you may be willing to accept such clients to help pay the bills or get some experience. Just be careful to not work for too low an hourly rate, or else the work is simply not worth your time.

It can be tempting to lower your fees significantly to get your first few clients. I would not advise doing this because raising your fees later is too difficult. If you continue working for the client, you will soon be resentful of the lower rates you are getting paid from the client. A better alternative would be to let the potential client know that $X is your normal fee or hourly rate. However, you are looking for some client testimonials to use on your website or as a reference, so you are willing to work for $Y for the first three or six months (or whatever). Doing this can help save your clients some money and convince them to give you a chance. Plus, doing this can provide you with a testimonial or review that you can use as advertising on your website or elsewhere. By using this method, you also let clients know that your fee will go up to your normal rate after a certain period of time.

On pages 153–54 is a list of questions to help when you are talking with potential or new clients. Remember to listen to their "pain points" (i.e., what problems prompted them to call for help?). Try to identify their needs and then let them know how you can help them.

Targeting a Niche

You do not have to select a specific niche or area of specialization when you are starting your business, but for many reasons thinking about a niche for your business may be a good idea.

One reason to specialize is that the rules and regulations and laws continue to change and are becoming increasingly complex. Only with difficulty can you keep current with all the requirements for payroll, income taxes, and the different laws for the different entity types, sales taxes, and possibly industry-specific rules and regulations that may apply to clients. Specializing makes it easier to keep current with the ever-changing laws for small businesses.

Another reason to develop a niche is that if you become known as an expert in your area of specialization, then you can usually charge higher fees. Plus, sometimes companies and small businesses want someone who is a specialist versus someone who is a generalist. Being a specialist can make attracting new clients and focusing your marketing efforts easier as well.

Specializing can also help you get referrals from other accounting professionals. If they know you specialize in a certain area, then they will not worry about you "stealing" their clients. This has been true for me. Because I specialize in QuickBooks consulting and training, other accountants feel comfortable when they refer their clients to me for help. They know that I do not do taxes (or monthly bookkeeping, etc.) and thus that I will not "steal" their clients. In return, I refer clients to them for tax preparation, etc. Similarly, I know some people who specialize in the retail industry (or whatever), so I may refer clients to them when the need arises.

In general, people usually choose to specialize based on the type of services provided or industries served. Let's discuss each one separately.

Services Provided

You may choose to specialize based on the services you provide. For example, H&R Block and Liberty Tax Service specialize in preparing income tax returns. Paychex, PayData, and others specialize in providing payroll services. Other firms may specialize in networking and technology, forensic accounting, cost segregation, or any number of other services. Specialization may not be the best choice for you when you are getting started, but as your business grows you may consider whether you would like to specialize in certain services.

When I started my home-based accounting business, I provided the typical accounting services. However, over the years I determined that I wanted to specialize in providing QuickBooks consulting and training services along with consulting, speaking, and writing. Thus I decided to quit providing payroll and tax services and instead developed referral relationships with other accounting professionals who provided those services. Because you are the boss, you can choose which services you want to provide.

Industry Specialization

Many people choose to specialize in one or more industries. Perhaps you have prior work experience in a certain industry or just an interest in an industry. Choosing an industry for your niche can really help you to focus on learning all the industry-specific laws and requirements for that industry. You may want to learn more about industry-specific software or programs, too. Some of the more common industries that people specialize in include:

- Contractors or construction: You can further specialize by focusing on homebuilders or remodelers, electricians, plumbers, or other specific trades. Job costing is important to them.
- Retail: This includes traditional retailers or e-tailers who need help integrating their website with an accounting or point of sale program.
- Restaurants: This industry has the continuous challenge of recording daily sales, monitoring inventory efficiently, dealing with frequent employee turnover, and paying a fair amount of bills.

- Manufacturing companies: They have specialized inventory needs.
- Nonprofit organizations: They need specialized reports, tracking of funds or grants, and reporting to their board of directors.
- Service-based businesses: These include attorneys, architects, engineers, etc. who need to track and bill for time and reimbursable expenses and other specialized needs.

Each of these industries represents an opportunity for specialization. They all have industry associations and specialized software for their industry, which can help you expand your services and work with larger clients. In later sections we will talk about identifying your target market to help focus your marketing efforts, and it is much easier if you choose an industry (or a couple of industries) for specialization.

Obtaining a Mailing or Contact List for Marketing

As you develop a marketing plan, obtaining a contact list or mailing list to help you target your marketing efforts is helpful. Perhaps you have heard of companies that sell a contact list or list of leads for hundreds or thousands of dollars. I will tell you how you can get your own list for free using a database called ReferenceUSA. Many public libraries purchase a subscription to ReferenceUSA, and library cardholders can access the database via the public library website.

Perhaps you want to do a direct mail campaign to attract more individuals for income tax return preparation. Using ReferenceUSA, you could do a search based on city or zip code, but the list may be too lengthy. So, assume you have identified a neighborhood that is in the income level you would like to target for potential clients. You need to have an address to enter, and then you can indicate that you want a list of all addresses within 1/10 mile or 2/10 mile—up to 1 mile around that initial address. You will get a list of all the addresses in the area indicated.

Another common use of ReferenceUSA is to create a contact list of certain businesses. You need to decide what types of businesses you would like to target. You can search for businesses based on many criteria, which you can specify, including the following:

- Size based on number of employees or sales volume
- Industry, such as contractors, plumbers, retailers, or florists; you can get as specific as you want
- Geographic area, either a greater metro area or zip code-specific

After you search and get your list, you can see a lot of information about an individual businesses. In addition to the name, address, and phone number of the business, much more information is provided. You can see the number of employees, sales volume, management names, and even a list of competitors. Having this contact information can help you contact potential clients and target your marketing efforts. I wrote an article about using ReferenceUSA to help explain how to search with it. You can read the article on pages 105-7.

Cultivating Referrals

For many years referrals have been the most effective marketing method for accounting professionals. Generally people do not want to find someone to do their bookkeeping, payroll, or taxes by looking in the Yellow Pages or advertisements. Because financial information is sensitive, people usually look for a referral from someone else. That is why, as accounting professionals, we need to network, network, and network some more, both locally and online, so we can develop relationships with others. We need to get to know people and let them get to know us so they will provide us with referrals. People want to do business with (or refer) people they know, like, and trust, and that is what we need to cultivate and develop.

So, how do you cultivate referral relationships? One of the first and easiest ways is to ask for referrals. Start with family members, friends, relatives, neighbors, and others you come into contact with during your daily life. Let them know that you have started your own business and tell them the services you provide and what types of clients you are looking for so they do not have to guess. Give them plenty of business cards and ask them to help you with starting your business.

Start networking with others in your community. Try to meet and get to know bankers, attorneys, insurance agents, real estate agents, other accounting professionals, and others who come in contact with small business owners or the types of clients you are targeting. Work on developing mutual referral relationships so you can refer clients to them as well.

Your networking and cultivating referrals should not just be in your local community either. You should also work on networking and building relationships online, which will be discussed in the next chapter.

Your current clients are a great source of referrals as well. Ask them if they are pleased with the work that you have been doing for them. They should say yes, or

Create Your Own Mailing or Contact List Using ReferenceUSA

Have you heard of Salesgenie, InfoUSA, USAData, or other sources where you can buy a mailing list or leads? Did you know some people have spent thousands of dollars buying lists from them to help get new clients? In this article I'll show you how you can create your own mailing or contact list for free using ReferenceUSA.

Perhaps you would like a list of manufacturing companies to contact. Maybe you are looking for new tax clients and would like to do a direct mailing to a certain neighborhood. Or maybe you want leads of businesses with more than a certain number of employees to see if they may be ready for QuickBooks Enterprise Solutions. Using ReferenceUSA, you can create your own list based on the criteria you specify.

What is ReferenceUSA, and how do I access it?

ReferenceUSA is "a premier subscription database available to libraries, educational institutions and government agencies." Many public libraries, schools, or universities have a subscription to ReferenceUSA, and many of them offer the option to access it remotely (from home with a library card). Here in Kansas City I can access ReferenceUSA via the Kansas City Public Library, Mid-Continent Public Library, Johnson County Public Library, or a community college or university.

All public libraries require a library card to access ReferenceUSA remotely. Some of the libraries will allow you to request and activate a library card online, and you do not necessarily need to be a resident to get a library card. For example, the Kansas City Public Library will issue cards to residents of Missouri and Kansas. So, the first step is to check with the public or school libraries in your area to see if they have a subscription to ReferenceUSA and then get a library card.

On the library website look for research resources or databases to find ReferenceUSA. You may want to check several libraries to see which ReferenceUSA databases they have. For example, the Kansas City Public Library has only three databases from ReferenceUSA: U.S. Businesses, Residential, and Healthcare, whereas the Mid-Continent Public Library has nine ReferenceUSA databases. The Mid-Continent Public Library includes the Canadian databases as well as One-Source (from which you can get the RMA Industry Averages and more) and one for New Businesses (possibly a great source of contacts or leads).

Searching with ReferenceUSA

Now that you've found a way to access ReferenceUSA, you can start searching. You need to know what you want a list of—residential addresses (perhaps for tax clients), new businesses, a certain type of business or industry (retailers, manufacturing, contractors, etc.), businesses with X number of employees or sales volume, businesses within a certain geographic area, etc. You should identify your target market to guide your search and provide good results.

If you use the residential database, you can search for home addresses within 1/10 mile or 1 mile of an address you enter. For example, I could enter my home address and get a listing of all my neighbors within the area specified. If you click on the custom search tab (as indicated below), you can create your own search form by checking the boxes that you want for the search criteria. Notice that you can search by median home value and median home income, too.

More importantly for many of us is the ability to search for businesses. Let's say I want to search for contractors (type of business) in my metro area (geographic) with one to four employees (size of business). As I check each search criterion, I get a search window to enter the relevant criterion.

First I'll search for the type of business. As I enter "contractors" into the field to look up, it will give me a list of results—I just click on the one(s) I want to select, and it puts it into the selected field.

I can add more search criteria to refine the results so I don't get too many. So, I'll search by metro area for the geographic area and one to four employees for the business size. When you check a field on the left, then a box opens on the right to enter the details for your search. After you have entered your search criteria, click on "view results" as indicated by the arrow.

When I view the results of the search, thirty names come up, which isn't too many, but perhaps I want more or fewer. If you click on "revise search," you can change some of the criteria to get more or fewer results.

If I revise the search for just a couple of cities (or zip codes), now I get only four results. Now you can download or print the results. You can click on "all" (as indicated with the arrow); however, because the service is free, you can download only twenty-five results at a time (one page of results). To download more than twenty-five, go to the next page and download them. It will put these results in a new file, so you will need to combine the files yourself.

When you click to download, you'll be able to select the file format and level of detail to download as shown below. If you need to download more than twenty-five results, then click on the back button to return to the search results and go to the next page.

When you are in the search results, if you click on the name of a company you will find a lot of information about the business. For example, you may want to know more about the business demographics, management, nearby businesses, or competitors. You can expand one or all of them.

The business demographics provide details about the number of employees, sales volume, number of P.C.s, and more. I don't think these data are totally accurate for all companies, but they can provide guidance for you.

If you're looking for contacts and leads, then you may want to look at the competitors for the businesses as well.

Now you have a tool to help you get contacts and leads whenever you need them for free. Spend some time identifying your target market to determine the search criteria you need to enter and start searching.

else you need to work on providing better service for them. Assuming they say yes, then ask them if they know others who could benefit from your services. Let them know that you would appreciate referrals.

Keep in mind how you present yourself to your clients and the impact that presentation can have on whether they provide you with referrals or not. One accounting professional was not getting any referrals, and so we were trying to determine the problem. Upon further discussions with her and her clients, we discovered the problem. She was trying to give the appearance of being busy and successful to her clients, which meant her clients did not want to provide referrals for her because they thought she was already too busy, and they feared her work for them might suffer. You do not want to give your clients the impression that you are too busy to handle their workload as well as any referrals they might provide.

What to Do with a Referral?

Suppose your client does give you the name of someone who might need your services. What do you do, and how do you handle the referral? You should contact the person (phone if possible) and say something along the lines of, "Hi. My name is Betty, and Joan Smith suggested that I give you a call. He thought I might be able to help you with your bookkeeping, taxes, payroll, or whatever." Then stop talking and listen. Sometimes listening is the most important aspect of talking with a potential client. You want to try to determine the person's pain points and what he needs and then tell him the benefits you can provide (not just the services you offer).

Finally, you should always follow up with the person who provided you with the referral. Let her know that you contacted the potential client and what happened. Thank her for the referral whether you get the client or not. If you get the client,

How NOT to Handle a Referral

Here is an example (all fictitious names and locations) of how *not* to handle a referral. A Certified ProAdvisor named "Betty Bookkeeper" from Boston had a client with an office in California who wanted someone local to help with installation and training on QuickBooks Enterprise Solutions (i.e., a larger client). Betty didn't know anyone in California, so she contacted me for a recommendation. I suggested she contact Cathy, who is a CPA and a Certified ProAdvisor in the area. However, when Betty contacted Cathy, Cathy was not very nice.

She was somewhat rude and condescending to Betty. Cathy told Betty to have the potential client contact her and to remind her how the potential client had gotten her name. In addition to being rude to Betty, it seemed as if Cathy could care less about the new potential client. Cathy should have taken the name and contact information of the referral and said she would be glad to contact the referral. Needless to say, Betty called me back and told me about Cathy's behavior and asked me for a different person as a referral. Obviously I will not provide any more referrals or recommendations for Cathy.

The other Certified ProAdvisor I recommended behaved much differently. She was nice and polite to Betty, gladly took the client's information, and said she would contact them right away to help. She followed up with me and Betty as to what happened with the potential client. Plus, she sent me a thank you note along with some brownies. Guess who will get more referrals in the future and will probably have a more successful business? This example also demonstrates why you should network with peers and get to know others at conferences or online.

sometimes a nice "thank you" gift would be appropriate. It can be a $5 or $10 Star-bucks gift card or even just a handwritten "thank you" note. A token of appreciation will help with future referrals. Even better is when you provide referrals for them, too.

Speaking or Presenting Seminars

Speaking or presenting seminars can be a great way to get referrals and potential clients. Just by being the speaker you are considered knowledgeable and have instant credibility. You want to make sure you focus on delivering the content of the presentation or seminar and not selling or promoting yourself. You could utilize a variety of presentations or seminars. Consider the type of client you are targeting.

Speak to Groups and Organizations

Speaking to industry groups or other organizations is a great way to reach poten-tial clients. You can create a reputation for yourself and work on networking and developing relationships with others. Local chambers of commerce and other orga-nizations are frequently looking for guest speakers for their monthly meetings. Or industry associations might need speakers for their meetings or conferences. When you are getting started and speaking locally, often these engagements will not be paid or will have minimal compensation. But they are a marketing method for you.

Consider what topics might be of interest to the group. Perhaps you could give the group an update on recent changes in the tax laws or other topics that may be of interest. Talk with someone from the group to determine who the audience will be and what topics would be of interest to them.

You should rehearse your presentation, but do not memorize it. Allow time for questions and answers. You might even have a few questions in mind in case no one asks something initially or give someone a question to ask you to break the ice. Make sure you arrive early and plan on staying afterward to network and answer any other questions. Have some handouts with your contact information included on it. Bring plenty of business cards and have them displayed conveniently for people to pick up. But remember that you are there to share your knowledge, not directly to sell or promote yourself.

QuickBooks Seminars

Teaching QuickBooks seminars is another way to reach potential clients. Although the attendees are coming to these seminars to learn about QuickBooks so they can do it themselves, they often discover they would rather pay someone to do it for them, or they need more help, training, or troubleshooting. When you teach the seminar, they get to know you, and you are "the expert" they are most likely to turn to for help. In addition, many seminar attendees may refer others to you. I have taught QuickBooks seminars for local Small Business Development Centers for the past ten years. I can tell you that doing so has been a great source of referrals for me, and it helps me learn more about QuickBooks as well. See the sidebar for more details.

A benefit of teaching for a Small Business Development Center or other organization is that these organizations do all the administration, registration, and marketing, provide the facility, etc. All I have to do is show up to teach the seminar. However, the compensation is not a lot, but teaching is marketing for me. Remember that you are there to teach the class, not to sell or promote yourself. But you will find that attendees often ask for your business card or pick it up if you leave it on the back table.

You may choose to offer QuickBooks seminars on your own. Doing this can be more work, but it can be more profitable as well. If you want to do this, you need to do all the administrative details, marketing, and registration, obtain a facility, etc. One issue to consider is whether or not you want to provide hands-on seminars at which each attendee works on a computer or whether you want to do a lecture/presentation type of seminar. Hands-on seminars can be better for attendees because they actually get to see the program and practice it. However, if some members of the group are slower than others, problems can arise. If you choose to do hands-on, you should limit the class size and ensure that attendees have a certain level of computer skills when they enroll in the seminar.

Intuit sells a site license for QuickBooks so you can purchase a ten-user or twenty-five-user site license for educational purposes. For details visit the website, http://accountant.intuit.com/training_cpe/intuit_education_program/qb_educator_resources.aspx. Also, as a ProAdvisor you have access to training materials. You can utilize PowerPoint slides, instructor's guide, and student handouts.

Teaching QuickBooks Seminars for a Small Business Development Center (SBDC)

I taught my first QuickBooks seminar for a local SBDC in 2000. The woman who was supposed to teach the seminar canceled a day before the class. When the director of the SBDC asked if I would teach it, I was scared and hesitant. I did not think I knew enough about QuickBooks to teach a seminar about it and with so little time to prepare. What if attendees asked questions that I could not answer? The director told me there was an instructor's manual and encouraged me to do it. I am so glad I agreed to teach that first seminar. I have taught QuickBooks seminars for that SBDC almost every month since then. From teaching these seminars, I have had countless clients and referrals over the years. Plus, the experience I gained from teaching so many QuickBooks seminars helped me become one of the few national trainers for Intuit. For the past several years, I have had the honor of teaching other accounting professionals about QuickBooks in live seminars nationwide and via webinars for Intuit Academy.

Seminars—Content and Timing

When I started teaching for the SBDC, one Introduction to QuickBooks seminar was offered—from about 9:00 a.m. to 4:00 p.m. for two days. It included inventory and payroll, which we discovered most attendees did not need. I also realized that a full-day session was too much information. The attendees were not learning anything after the first several hours of the day.

Over the years we refined the seminar and added new ones. We decided to offer payroll as a separate seminar for those people who needed it. We revised the Introduction to QuickBooks course to be two half-days to avoid the information overload of an all-day seminar.

The seminars have always been hands-on, with each attendee working on a computer. We had an educational site license from Intuit, so all attendees were on the same version of QuickBooks using the same sample file (except for the intermediate workshop). The seminars currently offered are as follows:

1. Introduction to QuickBooks—six to eight hours over two half-days (Tuesday/Thursday)
    - Interview and overview
    - Working with lists
    - Sales and payables cycles
    - Reconciliations
    - Sales taxes
    - Reports
2. Intermediate workshop—three to four hours
    - Smaller class size
    - Topics based on needs of attendees
3. Payroll—two hours
4. Jobs, Time, and Mileage—two hours

   I started with the instructor's manual that is available to members of the Pro-Advisor program and modified it over the years. (ProAdvisor members can log in to http://proadvisor.intuit.com; in the "Training" section the manual is in the "Train Your Clients" materials to download.) After teaching the introduction to QuickBooks seminar monthly for so long, I have memorized it and all the examples and exercises. Having done this allows me to add or eliminate topics as needed based on the level of participants in the seminar.

Lessons Learned

Over the years I have learned a few lessons. Among them are:

- You must control the crowd—you cannot let one person ask all the questions, slow it down, or whatever. Learn to "put it in the parking lot" for later discussion or talk with the person individually during a break or after class.

- People will ask lots of questions, and you will not know the answer to them all. This is how you learn more about QuickBooks. Tell people you will find out the answer and follow up with them later.

- Pass out your business card and tell people to contact you if they get home and realize they have a quick question that they forgot to ask. This is a low-key way to distribute your business card and make sure people have your contact information.

- Find out attendees' businesses at the beginning so you can tailor examples to their businesses.

- Anticipate problems and be able to laugh it off or continue with the seminar. Equipment problems, interruptions, or other events will disrupt the seminar, and you need to deal with them calmly and professionally.

Benefits of Teaching Seminars

I get paid for teaching the seminars, although the pay is much lower than my normal billing rate. However, teaching is a marketing method for me and a good source of referrals and new clients. The questions from seminar attendees help me learn more about QuickBooks and the needs of different industries. Plus, I really enjoy teaching "newbies" the right way to do things in QuickBooks so they can avoid some of the most common mistakes.

08

Online Marketing and Social Media

In order to run a successful business, you should establish an online presence, and you need to work on online marketing, social media, and social networking. The traditional marketing methods are not enough anymore, and the online method can be just as important or even more important than traditional methods.

Your Website

Hopefully by now you realize that you must have a website. Potential clients and other people you meet will look for you and your business online. They will be looking for your website to learn more about your business. Nowadays having a website—and an online presence in general—is just as essential (and maybe even more essential) to your business as having business cards.

In a previous section on selecting a name for your business, we discussed determining if the domain name was available. Hopefully you have purchased a domain name (URL) for your business. If not, the first step is to buy a domain name from one of the many companies that sells them.

Next you will need to find a company to host your website (i.e., this company will host the site on its servers so others can access it) and decide how to design and maintain the site. We will discuss several options for you to consider. Most of the free or low-cost options provide all three services: domain name, hosting, and site design. With some of the other options available (to be discussed below), you may use other tools to create and design the website, but you will need someone to host it and to register the domain.

Consider what type of website you want and how much you can spend. You may want (or need) to start out with a smaller, less-expensive website (note: that does not mean it should look unprofessional). Then, as your business grows (and your finances improve), you can update your site over time. We will discuss how you can create a basic, brochure-type website and have it hosted for free or for relatively low cost. Then we will discuss some companies that will create and host a site for you, complete with lots of content on it (which, by the way, is a more expensive option).

Basic Requirements for Your Website

For your home-based bookkeeping business, your website will most likely be more of an informational, brochure-type site compared with a site that requires an online shopping cart. At a minimum your site should include a homepage, a list of the company's services, an "About Us" page, and a "Contact Us" page. These days people commonly look at your website to learn more about you and your business before approaching you directly.

A picture is important. People want to know who you are, and a picture of yourself on your site is a way for them to get to know you. Remember that people do business with people they know, like, and trust, and a picture helps tremendously. The picture does not have to be one from a professional photographer. I suggest limiting the photograph to just your head and shoulders (like a portrait shot) so potential clients and others can see you. Make sure that your face is lighted (no shadows) and that the background is somewhat neutral (or at least not distracting). Also be sure you are wearing professional attire, business casual, or something that represents the image you want to convey.

Obviously you want to provide details about the services you offer (as was discussed in a previous chapter). You don't have to list every task you can perform for monthly bookkeeping services. Instead, focus on the benefits that you provide for clients—many of whom are small business owners. Make it easy for potential clients to get an idea of the services and benefits you provide, but try not to limit yourself either (at least try not to do so initially when you need work). Have other people help you with writing and editing your site, and remember to consider your site's script from the perspective of potential clients. Focus on their needs, the benefits that they are looking for, and the "pain points" that you can eliminate for them.

The "About Us" page should include some information about yourself; be sure to keep it relevant and professional. Provide information about your education, training classes, or certifications. In addition, details about relevant work experience and qualifications can help establish your credentials. This is where you establish yourself as a professional who is serious about your business. Do not forget to list any awards, recognition, or other accomplishments. Include any publicity that you may have received, including press notices or quotes in articles or the media, guest speaker appearances, or other achievements that can enhance your reputation. Sometimes doing this feels somewhat awkward, but this is where you need to brag about yourself. Establish your qualifications.

You definitely need a "Contact Us" page on your site. Make it easy for potential clients or others to reach you by phone or e-mail at a minimum. You can include a physical address; however, you may choose not to because you are home-based. Instead, you may decide to list just the city and state instead of a street address. Do you want to include your cell phone number or just an office number? Maybe you want to include your cell phone number with a comment that it is for "emergencies only." But then you need to worry about what constitutes emergencies. I would suggest not including your cell phone number on your site and instead giving it out to only established clients. You may want to list "office hours" for calls to protect your personal time. Having clients fill out a "Contact Us" form that, once submitted, will

Search Engine Rankings

When people use Google to search, they get pages and pages of results. Being on the first page, at the top of the search results, is highly coveted and desirable. If you rank high in the search results, then potential clients are more likely to find you. Some businesses buy Google Ad words to be listed on the right side of the search results (they pay a certain amount every time someone clicks on their link).

Some people say they can "guarantee" that you will be on page one of the search results if you pay them for their search engine optimization (SEO) services and consulting. However, no one knows the exact algorithm for Google search, and no one can truly guarantee search ranking.

You should use keywords, update your content frequently, link to other websites, have backlinks from other quality websites to yours, etc. to help improve your search engine ranking. Doing so can take some time, so be patient and persistent in your efforts.

send you an e-mail is nice. However, this form is not required on your site as long as you provide your e-mail address.

Consider including client testimonials, reviews, or comments on your website. Potential clients like to read what others have to say about you and your work, and testimonials help to enhance your credibility. The testimonials or comments do not have to be long. They can suffice even at just a sentence or two. Ask clients if they would be willing to provide you with a testimonial for your website. Many clients would be happy to help. However, they may not know what to say, so you can offer to write a couple of things for them to modify or approve. Ask them if you can include their name and perhaps a link to their business website as well. Doing this can really be a win-win for both of you because linking to their site will help with the search engine ranking of their website as well as provide more exposure for their business.

You probably should include a privacy policy and terms of service on your website. Samples of both are provided on pages 118–21 or you can find samples online to customize for your site.

Spend some time looking at the websites of other accounting professionals from the eyes of potential clients. Make notes about what you like or do not like. What information would you like to see, what is missing, and what is unnecessary "fluff" on their sites? Doing this can help you to create a better website for yourself.

Free or Low-Cost Options

Your website should present a professional image. Do not have any misspellings or poor grammar, and do not use clip art, which can come across as somewhat cheesy and unprofessional. When you are starting out, you do not need to spend a lot of money on a website. Free and low-cost options for your website design are out there. If you can use Microsoft Publisher to create cards or other things, then you should be able to use the templates available to create a basic site for your business. If you need help, you could contact marketing students or graphic artists from a local community college who would most likely be able to create a site for you without costing you lots of money.

Microsoft Office Live

You can get a free website from Microsoft Office Live to get you started. Microsoft Office Live offers a free domain name, but note that this name ends with ".officelive

Website Terms of Service and Privacy Policy

Terms of Service

Welcome to our website. If you continue to browse and use this website, you are agreeing to comply with and be bound by the following terms and conditions of use, which together with our privacy policy govern Long for Success, LLC's relationship with you in relation to this website. If you disagree with any part of these terms and conditions, please do not use our website.

The term "Long for Success, LLC" or "us" or "we" refers to the owner of the website whose registered office is in Lee's Summit, Missouri. The term "you" refers to the user or viewer of our website.

The use of this website is subject to the following terms of use:

- The content of the pages of this website is for your general information and use only. It is subject to change without notice.

- Neither we nor any third parties provide any warranty or guarantee as to the accuracy, timeliness, performance, completeness, or suitability of the information and materials found or offered on this website for any particular purpose. You acknowledge that such information and materials may contain inaccuracies or errors, and we expressly exclude liability for any such inaccuracies or errors to the fullest extent permitted by law.

- Your use of any information or materials on this website is entirely at your own risk, for which we shall not be liable. It shall be your own responsibility to ensure that any products, services, or information available through this website meet your specific requirements.

- This website contains material that is owned by or licensed to us. This material includes, but is not limited to, the design, layout, look, appearance, and graphics. Reproduction is prohibited other than in accordance with the copyright notice, which forms part of these terms and conditions.

- All trademarks reproduced in this website are the property of their respective owners and are not the property of, or licensed to, the operator. Intuit, the Intuit logo, QuickBooks, QuickBooks Pro, QuickBooks Premier,

QuickBooks Enterprise Solutions, ProAdvisor Program, and others are registered trademarks and/or registered service marks of Intuit Inc. or one of its subsidiaries in the United States and other countries.

- Unauthorized use of this website may give rise to a claim for damages and/or be a criminal offense.

- From time to time this website may also include links to other websites. These links are provided for your convenience to provide further information. They do not signify that we endorse the website(s). We have no responsibility for the content of the linked website(s).

- Your use of this website and any dispute arising out of such use of the website are subject to the laws of the United States.

- Any rights not expressly granted herein are reserved.

- Other brands or product names are trademarks or service marks of their respective owners, should be treated as such, and may be registered in various jurisdictions.

- The names of actual companies and products mentioned herein may be the trademarks of their respective owners. The example companies, organizations, products, people, and events depicted herein are fictitious. No association with any real company, organization, product, person, or event is intended or should be inferred.

Privacy

To Our Individual Clients

Your privacy is important to us, and maintaining your trust and confidence is one of our highest priorities. We respect your right to keep your personal information confidential and understand your desire to avoid unwanted solicitations. A recent law change requires us (along with banks, brokerage houses, and other financial institutions) to disclose our privacy policy to you—which we are more than happy to do. We hope that by taking a few minutes to read it, you will have a better understanding of what we do with the information you provide us and how we keep it private and secure.

A. Types of Information We Collect

We collect certain personal information about you—but only when that information is provided by you or is obtained by us with your authorization. We use that information to prepare your personal income tax returns and may also provide various tax and financial planning services to you at your request.

Examples of sources from which we collect information include:

- interviews and phone calls with you,

- letters or e-mails from you,

- tax return or financial planning organizers, and

- financial history questionnaires.

B. Parties to Whom We Disclose Information

As a general rule, we do not disclose personal information about our clients or former clients to anyone. However, to the extent permitted by law and any applicable state code of professional conduct, certain nonpublic information about you may be disclosed in the following situations:

- To comply with a validly issued and enforceable subpoena or summons.

- In the course of a review of our firm's practices under the authorization of a state or national licensing board or as necessary to properly respond to an inquiry or complaint from such a licensing board or organization.

- In conjunction with a prospective purchase, sale, or merger of all or part of our practice, provided that we take appropriate precautions (for example, through a written confidentiality agreement) so the prospective purchaser or merger partner does not disclose information obtained in the course of the review.

- As a part of any actual or threatened legal proceedings or alternative dispute resolution proceedings initiated either by or against us, provided we disclose only the information necessary to file, pursue, or defend against the lawsuit and take reasonable precautions to ensure that the information disclosed does not become a matter of public record.

- To provide information to affiliates of the firm and nonaffiliated third parties who perform services or functions for us in conjunction with our services to you, but only if we have a contractual agreement with the other party that prohibits that party from disclosing or using the information other than for the purposes for which it was disclosed. (Examples of such disclosures include using an outside service bureau to process tax returns or engaging a records-retention agency to store prior year records.)

C. Confidentiality and Security of Nonpublic Personal Information

Except as otherwise described in this notice, we restrict access to nonpublic personal information about you to employees of our firm and other parties who must use that information to provide services to you. Their right to further disclose and use the information is limited by the policies of our firm, applicable law, our code of professional conduct, and nondisclosure agreements where appropriate. We also maintain physical, electronic, and procedural safeguards in compliance with applicable laws and regulations to guard your personal information from unauthorized access, alteration, or premature destruction.

Thank you for allowing us to serve your accounting, tax, and financial planning needs. We value your business and are committed to protecting your privacy. We hope you view our firm as your most trusted advisor, and we will work to continue earning your trust. Please call us if you have any questions or if we can be of further service.

.com," which is not very professional. You can register your own domain name with Microsoft Office Live. The cost is about $15 per year after the first year (which is free). I encourage you to research the Microsoft Office Live website, which provides details of what you get with Microsoft Office Live Small Business Services.

The free website from Microsoft Office Live includes 500 megabytes of free storage space, which would be more than sufficient for your site initially. You can buy additional storage space when you need it. Plus, the other features are very affordable. For example, if you choose premium e-mail (without advertisements), the cost is about $20 per year.

Note that when you use the free website and hosting from Microsoft Office Live, an automatic message, "Powered by Microsoft Office Live," appears at the bottom of the website. But that is not that big of a deal, and many people may not even notice it. If you design a professional-looking site, then this small detail may not matter at all. The price is definitely right, especially if you are on a tight budget and this service is easy to use to create your own website.

Intuit Websites

The Homestead company provided website design, hosting, and more for small businesses and was known for letting people easily create their own websites. Intuit purchased Homestead, and it is now called "Intuit Websites." Intuit Websites offers more than two thousand professionally designed templates, which you can use to help you get started with your website. Then you can customize it with graphics (the service has a library of 250,000 images to choose from, or you can use your own), your own text, and other customizations. You will have your own domain name and e-mail address as well. Designing your own site and updating it with the tools provided by Intuit Websites are easy. If you have questions or need help, the company offers web advisors to help you. You could have them create the website for you if you want to pay about $600 to $1,000.

After creating the website, you have to pay a monthly hosting fee. The basic hosting plan from Intuit Websites is about $5 per month ($60 per year, which is not much). However, you probably will want to get the business hosting plan. The business hosting plan includes your domain name and e-mail address, which are not included in the basic hosting plan. The business hosting plan is about $20–$25 per month or about $240–$300 per year.

GoDaddy.com or Other Hosting Companies

GoDaddy.com is just one of many companies that provides web hosting and website design services. The principles discussed here would apply to other hosting companies as well. GoDaddy offers a variety of options for registering a domain name, hosting your site, and working with website builders.

With GoDaddy or another hosting company, you need to consider how you will design the site. Will you do it yourself, or will you have someone else design it, with you updating and maintaining it? You can create your own website and upload it for hosting by GoDaddy (i.e., it will be on GoDaddy's servers). You can purchase and use desktop programs, such as Microsoft Publisher and Dreamweaver, to create your site. Then you can upload it to the hosting company's servers.

You also can use online programs (many of them free) to create a website. Some popular ones include WordPress and Joomla. Plus, many templates (free or purchased) are available to get your site started. Numerous plugins or widgets (usually free) are available to help enhance your website quickly and easily. If you design the site yourself, then you need just web hosting.

Another option is to use GoDaddy's website design or site builder, called "Website Tonight." Website Tonight has over fifteen hundred templates and eight thousand images that you can use, and it is easy to use and edit. However, you need to watch the page limits with this option. If you have more than five pages, then you need to invest in Go Daddy's deluxe or premium plans. The chart below provides a comparison of the options and prices from GoDaddy (however, prices and terms may change and vary since this publication).

If you want just website hosting, then the economy plan will be sufficient for most home-based bookkeeping businesses. If you opt for Website Tonight, then you may need to upgrade your subscription as your website grows to more pages. You may want to consider several other add-on services offered by GoDaddy. However, do not purchase a lot of additional services initially. You may find many of the features (such as website statistics and blogs) elsewhere for free.

	Web Hosting— Economy	Website Tonight— Economy	Website Tonight— Deluxe	Website Tonight— Premium
Page Limits		5	10	999
Space	10 GB	50 MB	2 GB	4 GB
E-mail addresses	100	1	500	1,000
1–3 months	$5/month or $60/year	$5/month or $60/year	$9/month or $108/year	$13/month or $156/year
24 months	$4/month or $48/year	$4.24/month or $51/year	$7.64/month or $92/year	$11.04/month or $132/year
36 months	$3/month or $36/year	$3.99/month or $48/year	$7.19/month or $86/year	$10.39/month or $125/year

Register Your Website

If you choose any of the free or low-cost options, then you need to register your website with Google and other search engines so people can find it. To register your site with Google, go to www.google.com/addurl/?continue=/addurl to submit your URL. Doing this will submit your site so Google will add it to its index the next time Google "crawls" the web. You should also register with Yahoo!, MSN, and Bing, which would cover over 90 percent of the search engines.

You can register at other sites to help maximize your search results and web exposure. Google Places is quick and easy to register at and can help your business get found in local search results. It is free, and you get a report periodically about the impressions, actions, and top search queries. Google Analytics is also free and provides a lot of statistics and information about your site traffic. Make sure to register for it as well.

You may hear a lot of talk about search engine optimization (SEO) and have people offer to create and optimize your website for lots of money. There are several things that you can do yourself to improve your search engine rankings. You can easily insert keywords and meta-data tags into your site for SEO using many of the website design templates that are available. Additionally, changing the content on your website (by writing blogs, as discussed next) and getting links to your site (by participating in community forums, as discussed later) can help improve your organic Google search results without costing you a lot of money. Besides, many clients do not find an accounting professional based off just a Google search. Plus, if you are a Certified ProAdvisor, your profile is already optimized for Google and other search engines.

Grade Your Website

You can see how your website is doing by using a free SEO tool called "Website Grader" (www.Websitegrader.com) or other similar websites that are available. It measures the marketing effectiveness of a website. It provides a score that incorporates factors such as website traffic, SEO, social popularity, and other technical factors. It also provides some basic advice on how the website can be improved from a marketing perspective. The Website Grader is a tool from HubSpot, an Internet marketing company. You will find a lot of other useful resources, free webinars, reports, and more on its website (www.hubspot.com).

My Website: Through the Years

For my first website I decided I needed to try building it on my own. As a FastTrac facilitator and coach helping people write a business plan and start their own business, I received a lot of questions about how to create a website. Often people would ask if they could do it on their own—entrepreneurs often have a very tight budget! I figured that the best way to learn more about creating a website would be to try it myself. Being an accountant, I am not a real "techie" or IT kind of person. I do all right, and I can create PowerPoint slides and cards with Microsoft Publisher. But could I create my own website?

I found a web-hosting company that provided a free program to help me create my own website without being too technical or knowing html. I spent many hours working on it (in hindsight, maybe it was not good use of my time), and I had a few problems along the way. I used the free support number to call about some problems I encountered, so having that available was helpful. I did create my own website, with several pages and graphics, too! I was very impressed with myself, and if I could do it, then I knew others could do it, too!

However, I did not update my website often, and the information became outdated fairly quickly. Because I had not used the web-hosting program for awhile, I was not very efficient when I tried to update the site. Having a static, out-of-date website was not very professional. In fact, it was probably worse than having no website at all for my business. So I knew I needed to update it.

I updated the site a few times after that, but I was not happy with the e-mail service provided by the web-hosting company. Many times the e-mails would bounce back or simply would not be delivered. The company seemed not to be keeping up with current technology. I became increasingly frustrated. It was time for a change.

Along with a new web-hosting company, I had a new business name and logo, which meant I definitely needed a new website, too! First I needed a program to use to create my website. I explored different content management system (CMS) programs and considered two of them—WordPress and Joomla. I didn't know much about either program and started reading the reviews and comments about them online. I had heard of WordPress, but someone said it was somewhat more powerful and complex, so I was afraid to try it. I decided to use Joomla to create my website. I spent many hours reading articles or watching videos about how to do things in Joomla to create a site. And voila! Finally I had a new website (after hours of my time). Again, I did not update it regularly, so I found that I could not remember how to use Joomla. I had to go back to the articles and videos to remember how to do things, and this process was not very efficient. I did not have the time or the patience anymore. I needed help.

I was also determined to have a website with a blog (see the section on blogging) that was easy for me to update and maintain. Based on what I had been reading, I knew it was time to switch to WordPress. However, I really did not have time to figure out how to customize a template, integrate the blog, fix the URLs, and include a contact form and other features that I wanted for my new, updated site. Luckily for me, I connected with a computer programmer (via Facebook) who wanted to start doing websites on his own. He was willing to help me out at reduced rates, and I was thrilled. He switched my website to WordPress and did all the things that I wanted and needed done. Best of all, I can update it and create blog posts easily. It took me a little while and several tries with other programs, but I feel like I finally have a "real" website!

Some lessons I learned:

- You can create your own website if you have the time—a lot of user-friendly tools and templates are available online to help.

- You do not have to spend a lot of money to get a site that looks professional.

- Update your website regularly; it helps with the site's search engine rankings, and you may forget how to perform updates if you do not do them often.

- Your website needs to evolve to keep up with your business and changes in technology, etc.

- At some point creating your own website is not a good use of your time. Price out how much your time is worth and consider if it may be time to pay someone else for her skills.

- Your website should project a professional image at all times. If it is stale and outdated, then your site may have an unprofessional look, which will reflect poorly on your business.

- Keep the website simple, clean, and professional. Focus on the client perspective and do not clutter the site with ads and other stuff that do not really add value.

Use the report from Website Grader to help you identify areas where you can improve the effectiveness of your site. How is the score for your blog? Maybe you need to create a blog or to blog more frequently. How are the inbound links for your site? If you answer questions in other community forums and groups, the links from your signature point back to your site. These inbound links help your site in the search engine rankings. You do not have to know a lot about Internet marketing or SEO to read the report and obtain some valuable information from it. Use it to help you improve your website. Read other sections of this book for more details about blogging, joining community groups or forums, using social media, and more because all of those components integrate to improve the effectiveness and ranking of your website.

Do You Need a Client Portal?

As you consider the needs of your accountant's or bookkeeper's website, you have another consideration: How are you going to exchange files and information with clients? QuickBooks files are often too large to send as e-mail attachments. You can use a file transfer service, such as Send This File or You Send It, or a file-sharing service, such as Dropbox. However, these services may not provide the security needed for your files. Of even more concern is the need to maintain the security of clients' Social Security numbers and sensitive financial information. A few states (Massachusetts and Nevada, for example) already require accountants to encrypt e-mails that contain personal information; other states are considering similar laws. As a result, many accountants, bookkeepers, and tax professionals are using client portals.

Client portals—secure online storage areas—can be used as an alternative to e-mail and as a way to upload large files that cannot pass through e-mail. A number of professionals use portals to receive source documents from clients and to post completed tax returns.

Many of the larger (i.e., more expensive) tax programs offer a client portal for firms with five hundred to one thousand clients or more. The cost for these client portals can be well over $1,000 per year. The good news is that you have lower-cost options when you are getting started and building up your client base. When selecting a client portal, you need to consider your company's security needs. An article in the *Journal of Accountancy* provided the following security guidelines to consider when selecting a portal vendor:

- 128-bit Secure Sockets Layer (SSL) encryption
- Nearly 100 percent network uptime (99.9 percent or more is typical)
- Regular, redundant data backup in case of a disaster

The article named two lower-cost options—both LeapFILE and ShareFile meet the suggested criteria for security. Both allow you to incorporate the portal into your website (i.e., a place where clients can enter their user name and password to access their files/folder) and provide support to get it set up. If you are just starting your home-based bookkeeping business, then the basic, or starter, plan would be sufficient to meet your needs. Those plans are around $20–$30 per month (or $240–$360 per year). A client portal provides many benefits and is becoming much more widely used and expected. If you do not have a client portal when you start your business, then you should consider getting one soon as you get more clients.

Other Website Options

Some other options for your website cost more; however, they provide numerous benefits. Several companies provide full-service websites for accountants. If you do not have the time or inclination to try to work on your site, then you may want to consider one of these companies. These companies provide a lot more than just a basic website, and many include most of the following:

- Content: A library of articles, FAQs, and financial guides on topics such as QuickBooks, taxes, investment strategies, and more
- Newsletters: E-mail monthly newsletters

- Financial calculators
- Blog
- Internet links
- Client portal

Although some people might think these services cost too much (most are $50 to $100 per month or $600 to $1,200 per year), these full-service websites really provide a lot of value, and you may want to consider one. However, when you are starting your home-based bookkeeping business, you may not have the funds. You may choose to start with one of the free or low-cost options, but as your business grows you may consider switching to a full-service website.

A full-service website has many benefits. A big benefit of having a website from one of these providers is having continuously updated content and e-mail newsletters. You would have difficulty finding the time to write articles and create a newsletter. Yet, keeping in touch with clients or potential clients with a regular newsletter is beneficial. Plus, these articles and content can help demonstrate your knowledge and expertise to clients, and these updates can help with search engine rankings. However, you should be careful that the articles do not misrepresent your skills or expertise.

Several companies, including CPA Site Solutions, Accountant Web Design, and ClientWhys, provide full-service websites. A good comparison of the many features, prices, and more of nine full-service website providers is found at www.Websites 4accountants.com, but you should do some of your own research and analysis as well. A full-service website may cost more than a basic site, but it provides many benefits. Plus, rather than spending your time trying to build your site yourself, you could be networking or doing other activities to build your business.

Writing Blogs or Articles

Writing blog posts or articles is a way for you to share information with your clients, potential clients, or peers and to demonstrate your knowledge and expertise. Getting started is really easy, but blogging on a regular basis does take discipline. Having a blog has many benefits, including the fact that it helps the search engine rankings of your website (if the blog is part of your site). Updating your content regularly helps your search engine results. Also, the keywords you use in your blog posts will show up in the search engine results. Keep this fact in mind as your write and use keywords and phrases that potential clients might use when searching for an accountant or bookkeeper. Write about topics so you can use these keywords and phrases. Consider who your ideal client is, what services you want to provide, and what industries you want to target. Write articles to help your target market of potential clients find you. Your blog posts also help establish your credibility and knowledge in an area. Be sure to provide useful and relevant information for potential or existing clients so they want to keep reading your blog. If you become a source of information for them, they will think of you when they need help, or if someone else needs help hopefully they will provide your name as a referral.

You can get started with a free blog in a matter of minutes. The most popular free blogs are hosted by Blogger (part of Google) and WordPress. With both you can choose a template or theme for the look of your blog. Blogger is much easier to get started with, whereas WordPress offers more capabilities and customization but is somewhat more technical. I started with Blogger but switched to WordPress, which was not as difficult as I feared.

I encourage you to incorporate your blog into your own website rather than use the free hosting. For example, if you use Blogger the URL is something.blogspot .com and not your domain or URL. The benefit of incorporating your blog into your website is that if you are updating your blog, the content of your site is changing. The search engines notice when the content of your site changes. Plus, all your blog posts will show up in the search results hopefully helping increase traffic to your website. Things to consider for an effective blog:

- Interactive—allows people to leave comments
- A variety of mediums—text, video, or links to other resources or blogs
- Reverse order—newest posts listed first

You may also want to write articles to submit to e-zines (online magazines) or other sites. Writing articles can help build your name recognition and reputation.

Using Social Media and Social Networking

Social media and social networking are not just a fad. Many people are making connections, developing relationships, and getting clients from online sources. Just as when you are offline, when you are online you are trying to network and develop relationships with others. You can "small talk" online just as you would at a chamber luncheon. Remember that people do business with people they know, like, and trust. You want to let them get to know and like you. Through the use

Social Media is for B2B and B2C

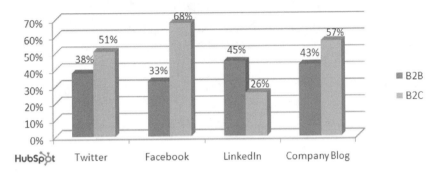

Percentage of Companies Using Specific Social Media Channels and/or Blogs Who Have Acquired a Customer From That Channel

Source: State of Inbound Marketing Report - http://bit.ly/aewfHr

of social media you can try to increase traffic to your site and/or blog. Do not do or say anything online that you would not do or say right in front of a potential client and be careful when posting photos of yourself, too. Your professional image and reputation are too important, so be sure that all photos and text are business-appropriate.

The chart above demonstrates how other companies use different forms of social media. You can see from looking at the chart the percentage of companies using specific social media channels or blogs, who have acquired a customer from the customer. For Business to Business (B2B), the highest percentage came from LinkedIn followed closely by the company blog whereas for Business to Consumer (B2C), it was Facebook followed by the company blog.

Tools can help you manage social media and social networks. These tools allow you to post something once and then update various sites, such as LinkedIn, Facebook, and Twitter. You can even schedule your posts. Some of the current tools are Ping. fm (http://ping.fm), HootSuite (www.hootsuite.com), TweetDeck (tweetdeck.com)

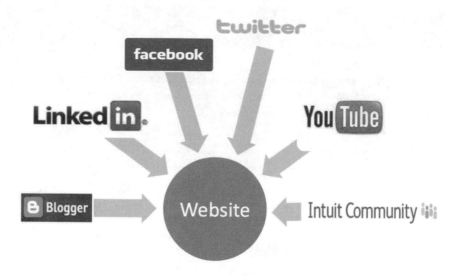

and SocialOomph (www.socialoomph.com), but new ones come along all the time. Google can help you find tools to help you efficiently manage your posts on various social media sites. Dashboards monitor feeds and various statistics, too. Remember to provide useful and relevant information that your clients or potential clients would be interested in with a few personal comments about what you are doing (such as presenting a seminar, being newly certified, etc.) as well.

Let's look at some of the most popular online social media and social networks for businesspeople. Remember that the ultimate goal is to drive traffic to your website.

LinkedIn

LinkedIn is widely used by businesspeople and small business owners. Your LinkedIn profile is like an online resume of your education and work experience. You can get recommendations (i.e. reviews) from others and provide information about yourself. Numerous groups and a question-and-answer forum provide you with an opportunity to demonstrate your knowledge and expertise. LinkedIn provides another opportunity for you to increase your name/brand recognition and to network with other people.

Many people use LinkedIn to search for someone with certain skills and expertise. Companies use it to find employees, and I have several clients who found me from LinkedIn.

One of the LinkedIn groups that I am a member of is the Mizzou Alumni Group (University of Missouri–Columbia). After going back to campus for a football game, I posted a comment in the LinkedIn group about how much the campus had changed and all the improvements. This post led to some good conversations with others who had moved away and appreciated the updates. One of the men in the discussion e-mailed me privately because he saw that my profile said I worked with Quick-Books. He needed some QuickBooks consulting and soon became a client, one whom I helped remotely. From our initial small talk about how the campus had changed—just the same as if we had been together at an alumni picnic—we connected, and I had a client from the discussion.

LinkedIn has brought me many business opportunities, and I encourage you to join LinkedIn and complete your profile.

Facebook

Whereas LinkedIn is primarily for businesspeople, Facebook is for everyone and tends to be more personal in nature. Facebook is an online tool that can help you with networking and building relationships with others. It is the most popular online social medium. Because it is more personal, I often hear people question how it can help them start and grow their business. It is just an online method to let family, friends, and relatives know that you are in business and would appreciate referrals. You do not need to post business-related items all the time, but an update once in awhile about something business related works great.

Reconnecting with classmates from high school or college is fun and can be a great source of clients or referrals for you. Some of them will be business owners (or will know others who are) who could use your services. Or they may be a source of referrals for you. For example, I reconnected with a guy from high school who is now an attorney. He and I both work with small businesses, and thus we can provide referrals for each other.

You should create a Facebook page for your business on which you can post more business-related information and links to useful information. When you write a blog post, make sure to include it on both LinkedIn and Facebook with a link back to your blog (i.e., website).

Twitter

Twitter has really increased in popularity and is widely used. Twitter is called "micro-blogging" because your posts (called "tweets") can be only 140 characters long. You need to learn to use keywords or phrases, abbreviate, and eliminate words that are not really necessary. People also use hashtags to help track and search for things. A hashtag is the pound sign followed by the keyword or phrase (#phrase).

When you post a link to your blog or an article that you want to share, the link is usually too long. You can use tools to shorten URLs. Two tools that are fairly common are bit.ly (http://bit.ly) and TinyURL (www.tinyurl.com). I like using bit.ly because it provides some statistics and information so you can see how many people clicked on the link. This feature can help you to see what people are interested in so that you can focus on those topics.

YouTube

Did you realize that YouTube is the second-largest search engine? People search YouTube for everything now! I wanted to know how to insert RAM into a notebook computer, and sure enough, YouTube had several videos that would show me how to do it. Drop an earring down your sink? YouTube videos show you how to get it out. Search for QuickBooks, and you will find lots of YouTube videos.

This capability is great for small business owners. In the past we could not afford commercials, and even professional videos were expensive. Now, with Flip videos, webcams, and more, you can create your own videos and upload them to YouTube in an afternoon.

Think about some topics that you could record that would be helpful to clients or potential clients. Maybe you want to record some QuickBooks tips or how-to videos. Maybe you want to make a video about the latest tax law changes, which may apply to them, or year-end tax strategies. What could you record to put on YouTube and your website that would provide useful and relevant information? Remember that doing this helps your search engine results and rankings as well. Plus, people can get to know you even better if they can see and hear you.

Several tools allow you to record your computer screen. Camtasia Studio is widely used and has many editing and other features. However, it costs about $300. Or, if you want to make shorter videos, free or low-cost tools are available. Jing (www.techsmith.com/jing) is from the same company that makes Camtasia Studio.

It is a free tool to record your screen and voice for up to five minutes. A pro version (for about $15 a year) allows you to record longer videos, has a better format for saving them, and a couple of other features.

If you want to record a video showing you (instead of your computer screen), then you want to use a webcam or a Flip video camera or something similar. You can buy a little tripod for the Flip video camera, too. Then you just flip out the USB port, plug the video camera into the computer, and upload your video directly to YouTube (or save it).

However you decide to make videos, you should try to make them as professional as possible. I have seen some with bad sound, background noise, dark lighting, blowing wind, or other distractions. Make sure that your face is lighted (if you are showing yourself) and that the sound is good with no background noises. Remember that such videos represent you and your business and are part of your brand image.

Write a blog post with keywords and phrases to help people find it when they are searching. Then include the video in your blog post (after you have uploaded it to YouTube). Doing this helps your website do better in the search engine rankings because you have new information and different forms of media (not just text but video, too).

Another suggestion is to record podcasts for people to download and listen to while commuting, exercising, or whatever. Podcasts are another form of social media that allows you to provide useful and relevant information in a format that meets the needs of some people.

Groups and Forums

The Internet has many groups and communities where people ask and answer questions and network with others: Google groups, Yahoo! groups, LinkedIn groups, and others. Plus, many community forums, such as the Intuit Community, exist. Think about your target market: What type of clients are you trying to reach, and what groups or forums would they frequent online? For example, if you want to focus on contractors, find some groups and forums for contractors where you can answer their questions or provide useful information for them to run their business. You want to develop your reputation as someone who provides relevant information and resources to help them. You want them to get to know, like, and trust you so when they need help, they will contact you.

When you join online groups or forums, sometimes it helps to listen in at first and get a feel for the groups. Then, when you start contributing, you always want to include a signature. Your signature should include your name, website, and any certifications or designations that you have earned. Including the link to your website provides an inbound link to your website from other sites. Doing this helps your search engine rankings. Plus, when people search for topics, often these discussions will appear in the search results, helping people to find and contact you. Participating on a regular basis over a period of time will really help with your website ranking and the search engine results of your answers and posts.

09

Financial Considerations (Including Pricing Services)

Financial considerations are an important part of building a successful business. Starting right includes considering start up costs and whether to begin part or full time. Determining your billing rates, how to track your time, and whether to use hourly or fixed fee rates is important. You should clarify your billing policies and terms as well as how to manage your expenditures.

Start-Up Costs

In previous chapters we discussed how to set up your home office, what things you need to start your home-based bookkeeping business, and some estimated costs. Now we will discuss ways to keep the costs down and bootstrap to get your business started. Even if you have some money saved, you may not want to go crazy spending a lot to start your business. It takes some time to build up a client base and steady income, so spend your money wisely.

Here we will review items based on their urgency—what you must have to get the business started, what would be nice to have, and what can wait until later. All of these were discussed in detail in other chapters.

Must have to start:

- Registration of your business and filing of the required forms with the Secretary of State
- Computer
- Accounting software
- Payroll and tax software if you will be providing those services
- Appropriate training (if you do not have it already)
- Business phone

Nice to have or can wait:

- Business cards
- Website
- Certifications
- Printer/copier
- Scanner
- Dual monitors
- High-speed Internet
- Other software (antivirus, Microsoft Office, etc.)
- Office furniture, fixtures, and supplies

Hopefully this list helps you to realize that if you already have the education and/or experience, then you do not have to spend a lot of money to get started. You may even have a computer or accounting software already. The actual start-up costs can be minimal because you are starting a service-based business.

One way to save money on the other items is to find used items at home, thrift stores, Craigslist, eBay, or other places that sell used office furniture, fixtures, and equipment. You can upgrade and buy more things as your business grows.

Full- or Part-Time?

If you are already working, then you may need to decide whether you should quit your job or start the business part-time. Your decision will depend on a few factors:

- Are you single or married or have a significant other?
- Do you have a family to support?
- Are you the sole provider, or does the household have another source of income?
- What about health insurance or other benefits?
- Do you have money in savings (preferably six to twelve months)?

You need to consider and discuss all these questions with your family. Building up a client base and having steady income take time. Starting the business part-time without leaving your current employment may be safer and easier from a financial standpoint. However, then you would probably be working long hours. If you have a full-time job, then finding time for the networking and marketing that you need to

Getting Clients in the Beginning

Getting the first clients is tough. Don't plan on your new business to provide a real income for a very long time, especially with the economy so troubled. You reinvest your earnings on your business—training, supplies, and advertising—before you have money to spend.

Rebecca Christiansen, Success Bookkeeping,
www.successbookkeeping.com, Redwood Valley, CA

When I started my business, I did three things, one of which I still do:

1. I put a flyer in the local *PennySaver* advertising my business with the motto, "Big or Small. We Do Them All."
2. I set up shop doing tax returns in a poor section of town.
3. And most importantly, I told everyone who came within 3 feet of me my name and a little bit about my business (this I still do).

Here's an example of what I said: "Hi, my name is Debbie Kilsheimer. I am the best bookkeeper in all of Volusia County and own the best accounting firm in the area. Do you know of anyone who could use a great bookkeeper and accounting firm? Here's my card."

People always took the card. And then a conversation would start. If you don't think you are the best at what you do, why should they? When was the last time you talked to an accountant/bookkeeper who was enthusiastic, friendly, and confident without being pretentious? People will remember you, and, when they need someone, they will call. And if they don't need you, be sure to tell them to hand your card to their friends. They do.

I walk into businesses and do the same thing. This practice works great and costs practically nothing. All it takes is courage, confidence, and guts. You will need these qualities to succeed in this business, above and beyond any accounting skills.

Debra Kilsheimer,
Behind the Scenes Financial Services, Port Orange, FL

do to get the business going is difficult. So, building the business may take longer if you are doing it part-time.

You may want to do some tasks on the side while you keep working. For example, you can form the business entity, get your EIN, set up a bank account, or work on the website while you continue working. Then, after you start getting a few clients, you may decide to quit.

Discuss the issue with your family and analyze the situation to decide what is best for your personal situation.

Billing Policies and Terms

Defining your billing policies, rates, and terms is one of the most difficult tasks you face when starting your business. Often this difficulty arises because of a lack of awareness of what is "normal" for the industry or average rates for your area or common practices for bookkeepers and accounting professionals.

Setting Your Billing Rates

Setting your initial billing rates is important and can be difficult. A common mistake is to set the initial billing rates too low. You could easily rationalize why your billing rates should be lower—because your home-based costs are lower or because you are new and just getting started and need to discount to attract clients, etc. Please do not set your billing rates too low. Increasing your rates later is difficult, and if you do not value your services, your clients will have difficulty seeing the value of your services.

If you think you need low billing rates to help get your first few clients, then you can put some alternatives into place rather than just setting low billing rates. For example, you can let a potential client know that your normal billing rate is $65 per hour. However, you are starting your business and need testimonials or reviews for your website or profile and will charge the client a discounted rate of $40 per hour for the first few months or something similar. The client knows that after the initial discount period your rates will increase, and yet he feels like he is saving some money, too.

You should consider many factors when setting your billing rates, and these factors are what make setting the rate difficult. Comparing your rates with those of someone else is difficult because of varying circumstances and factors, but average billing rate surveys can help. Intuit's Average Billing Rates Survey from 2009 provides

Intuit Average Billing Rates Survey 2009

January 2010—Slow Rates Growth

(This article is reprinted in its entirety with permission from Intuit.)

Intuit conducted a nonscientific QuickBooks rates survey last year and saw most rates creep up slightly from 2007, with few exceptions.

Intuit's 2009 Rates Survey shows relative gains for Certified ProAdvisors. The difference between rates charged by Certified QuickBooks ProAdvisors and uncertified ProAdvisors has never been greater. Since 2007 rates for Certified ProAdvisors rose by seven percent; during the same period, rates for uncertified ProAdvisors actually declined.

Category of Bookkeeping Rate

While we asked about various hourly services, we are using hourly bookkeeping rates to provide a thumbnail sketch of the changes between 2009 and 2007. The 2007 rates are shown in parentheses, followed with the percentage change.

- All Respondents $64 ($61) 5%

- **Certified QuickBooks ProAdvisors $64 ($60) 7%**

- QuickBooks ProAdvisors (Uncertified) $56 ($59) -5%

- All QuickBooks ProAdvisors $63 ($60) 5%

- All ProAdvisors Who Are Not CPAs $58 ($53) 9%

- All ProAdvisors Who Are CPAs $75 ($68) 10%

- All CPAs $77 ($71) 8%

- Bookkeepers $55 ($48) 15%

As shown in the "bookkeepers" category, the most pressure for rates to increase comes from the lower end of the spectrum. After that, the subset of ProAdvisors who are also CPAs saw the highest increases overall.

Average versus Mode. Because most practitioners charge round figures, the statistical mode (the value that is used most frequently) across all accounting professionals is $50 for bookkeeping and $75 for other services.

Hourly Rates Overview Table—All Respondents

Response	General Book-keeping	Generating Reports	Software Install/ Setup	Trouble-shooting	Training	On-site Mainte-nance	Telephone Consulting	General Business Consulting
Count	443	423	409	426	405	353	424	422
Average	$64	$74	$83	$79	$80	$79	$79	**$95**
Mode (Most Frequent)	$50	$75	$75	$75	$75	$75	$75	$75

The average amount for **general business consulting** is shown above in boldface because it is the only rate that came in lower than in 2007 (averaged across all practitioners). The mode for general business consulting was $75 in both 2007 and 2009.

Fixed Fees Overview Table—All Respondents

Response	Installation and Setup (New User)	Generate Statements	Quarterly Tune-up	Personal Training (1–2 Hrs.)	Personal Training (3–4 Hrs.)	Personal Training (Full Day)
Count	138	127	128	115	109	100
Average	$327	$251	$231	$159	$303	$572
Mode	$500	$250	$250	$150	$300	$500

Hourly Rates Overview Table—All QuickBooks ProAdvisors

Response	General Book-keeping	Generating Reports	Software Install/ Setup	Trouble-shooting	Training	On-site Mainte-nance	Telephone Consulting	General Business Consulting
Count	386	368	357	372	354	307	370	369
Average	$63	$82	$72	$78	$79	$78	$80	$86
Mode (Most Frequent)	$50	$75	$50	$75	$75	$50	$75	$50

Fixed Fees Overview Table—All QuickBooks ProAdvisors

Response	Installation and Setup (New User)	Generate Statements	Quarterly Tune-up	Personal Training (1–2 Hrs.)	Personal Training (3–4 Hrs.)	Personal Training (Full Day)
Count	104	93	99	93	88	79
Average	$310	$246	$225	$160	$305	$565
Mode	$500	$250	$250	$150	$300	$500

Hourly Rates Overview Table—Certified QuickBooks ProAdvisors

Response	General Book-keeping	Generating Reports	Software Install/ Setup	Trouble-shooting	Training	On-site Mainte-nance	Telephone Consulting	General Business Consulting
Count	237	235	222	233	223	190	232	227
Average	$64	$84	$75	$81	$82	$81	$82	$87
Mode (Most Frequent)	$50	$75	$75	$75	$75	$75	$75	$75

Fixed Fees Overview Table—All QuickBooks ProAdvisors

Response	Installation and Setup (New User)	Generate Statements	Quarterly Tune-up	Personal Training (1–2 Hrs.)	Personal Training (3–4 Hrs.)	Personal Training (Full Day)
Count	82	68	77	73	68	59
Average	$331	$265	$235	$166	$318	$573
Mode	$500	$150	$250	$150	$300	$500

Hourly Rates Overview Table—QuickBooks ProAdvisors (Uncertified)

Response	General Book-keeping	Generating Reports	Software Install/ Setup	Trouble-shooting	Training	On-site Mainte-nance	Telephone Consulting	General Business Consulting
Count	62	59	57	59	57	48	59	58
Average	$56	$80	$64	$69	$72	$68	$72	$80
Mode (Most Frequent)	$50	$75	$50	$50	$75	$50	$75	$50

We did not receive enough responses on fixed fees from uncertified QuickBooks ProAdvisors to list results for this subgroup.

Notes

1. Intuit conducted this informal survey May through July 2009. The results are shared for reference only as one data input among many for practitioners reviewing their current rate structure. Readers are cautioned that although we believe the results to be generally accurate and useful, the survey is informal and unscientific, as it's open to all practitioners via Internet access and there is no screening or verification of results. Intuit began conducting such surveys in response to frequent requests from QuickBooks bookkeepers and accountants. The previous survey to the 2009 survey was conducted in 2007; there are no figures for 2008.
2. The "Bookkeeper" category consists of all practitioners except for all QuickBooks ProAdvisors and CPAs.

Bill Teague is managing editor of the Intuit ProConnection *newsletter and website. For many years he was an editor and associate publisher at Harcourt Professional Publishing, which published* CPA Digest, Tax Accountants Weekly, *and other publications for accountants.*

Last Updated: 01/29/2010

insight. According to this survey, the national average billing rate for bookkeepers was $55 per hour, whereas Certified QuickBooks ProAdvisors reported an average billing rate of $64 per hour. Billing rates can vary based on many factors, including:

- Education
- Experience
- Certifications and designations
- Industry expertise
- Geographic location

Watch out for potential clients who are looking for someone who charges the lowest rate. Typically they will not be good clients for you (they always complain, do not get the information you need, are disorganized, and can simply be a pain). These clients will leave when they find someone else at a lower rate. When you are just starting your business, you might find it hard to believe that you are better off without some clients. You do not have to accept every client who contacts you.

Hourly or Fixed Fee

In addition to determining your hourly billing rate you should consider how to bill your clients. You may decide to charge hourly for some projects but charge a fixed fee for other projects. If you can charge fixed fees, then you may be more profitable than if you charged only hourly. When you are trying to decide whether to bill hourly or a fixed fee, each method has several pros and cons.

Hourly Billing Rates

Pros:

- They are easy both for clients to understand and for you to bill.
- You get paid for the time you work.
- They are good for cleaning up messes when you do not know how long it will take.

Cons:

- Client may question your high hourly rate.
- Does the time count when you take a quick break?
- Do you need to account for the work performed in detail?
- The client may be afraid to call or ask questions if you are "on the clock."
- Client may not be happy to receive an unexpected high bill.

Fixed Fees

Pros:

- Client knows how much the work will cost and can budget accordingly.
- You have no need to track every minute working on the project (although you should to see the actual time involved).
- Profitability improves as you improve efficiency.

Cons:

- Gauging the amount of time projects will take is difficult.
- The unexpected can occur.

The good news is that you do not have to use just hourly or just fixed fees—you can use both. For example, if you are cleaning up a messy QuickBooks data file or entering six months of transactions for a client, then you may want to charge an hourly rate. On the other hand, if you are preparing the payroll on a regular basis or doing monthly bookkeeping, then you may want to set a fixed fee for the work. You may want to work with a client on an hourly basis for a period of time to see how long the work actually takes and then come up with an amount for a fixed fee. With more experience, you can more easily estimate and set fixed fees.

Track Your Time

Whether you decide to use hourly billing rates or fixed fees, you should have a method to track your time. You have several options for tracking your time depending upon your personal preference. Some people like to use Outlook, the QuickBooks Timer, another timer program, a stopwatch app on their phone, or the traditional handwritten timesheet. You should choose a method that works for you and that you will use to record your time.

Billing Policies

You will need to determine how you will bill clients and establish billing policies. Your policies may vary depending on whether the client is an ongoing, monthly client or a consulting or training client. Sometimes you may send the client an invoice, and he will remit payment later. However, in some situations (for example, you enter several months of history or clean up a messy QuickBooks file), you are wiser to get a retainer from the client up front. For example, you may ask her to pay you for five or ten hours (or whatever amount is appropriate depending on the size of the project) up front as a retainer. Then, as you work off that amount you should collect from her again. Doing this prevents you from doing all the work and the client not wanting to pay you for it, and it also prevents the client from getting one big bill when the work is complete.

As part of your billing policies, consider whether you will bill for travel time. Some people bill travel time at 50 percent of their normal billing rate or have a minimum

Time Is Money

For clients I assist on-site I log the hours I work in my planner, which is with me at all times. When clients are billed, I reference the date and hours worked on the invoice.

For remote clients who prefer detailed bills, I have a basic form (as shown below) kept at the front of their binder to track hours and tasks. This is invaluable to me as a time tracker as well as a basis for invoice detail, since I tend to spend a few hours here and there on remote clients rather than a big chunk of time once or twice a month. Furthermore, I've learned to record time spent on phone calls and e-mails on this form since many tend to be lengthy. At the time of invoicing I can reference significant e-mails and phone calls for billing purposes or provide a line item for the sum of e-mails and phone calls in that billing period.

Date	In	Out	Task	Invoice Number
Aug 12	12:00	1:00	Monthly Sales Tax	4528

Beth Damis, Bookkeeping by Beth, LLC, Mill Creek, WA

charge for going on-site to the client's location. For example, I prefer to work with clients remotely instead of driving all over town and getting stuck in traffic. I established a two-hour minimum charge if clients want me on-site at their location. This charge encourages clients to set up remote meetings for quick questions or training. I am able to meet with many more clients throughout the day when I work remotely compared with when I am driving all over town.

Another consideration is whether you will bill clients for quick questions via phone or e-mail. You should evaluate the time you will spend tracking the five to ten minutes spent and invoicing for the time versus encouraging the client to ask quick questions without fear of being charged for it. Personally, I do not want to try to track the time, and I think answering quick questions "off the clock" generates goodwill with my clients. I have found that most of my clients do not abuse the quick questions. If a client is asking too many questions, then it usually indicates that he needs more help or training and that you should schedule a meeting with him (which is billable).

Manage Accounts Receivable and Collections

Managing your accounts receivable and not letting a client get too far behind are important. If the client is not paying you, then you should stop doing the work. Stay on top of accounts receivable at all times—you deserve to be paid for your work! We discussed collecting a retainer from clients, and you may get paid when the work is performed as well. These are great methods to ensure that you receive payment. You should also ensure that you invoice clients promptly for the services provided.

Accept Credit Cards or Online Payments

Increasing numbers of accountants and bookkeepers are accepting credit card payments and online payments from clients. Several options are available, and clients are more comfortable making online payments than in the past. When you are starting out you may want to use just PayPal, which would allow clients to pay you with a credit card or e-check with no monthly charges. You can accept e-checks from clients using Intuit PaymentNetwork (http://paymentnetwork.intuit.com) for only fifty cents per transaction and no monthly charges.

As your business grows, you may want to consider other options. For example, if you have a lot of recurring billings for monthly services or payroll, then you may want to set up automatic payments. You may use a merchant service, such as Intuit's Merchant Services, to accept credit cards in a variety of methods. For example, I have used Intuit Billing Solutions, which allows me to invoice a client, who can then click a link in the e-mail to pay the bill securely online. Or perhaps you want to accept credit cards when you are at the client location using something like Intuit GoPayment. Numerous options exist, and they all help you collect your fees more quickly and easily.

Efficient Billing Policies and Procedures

Most of the clients of our full-service bookkeeping company are on monthly retainers. We quote our clients based on what services we provide for them and require that the monthly fee is paid at the first of the month, either via an automatic recurring credit card transaction or an e-check we manually receive. By billing this way, my staff and I spend less time chasing money from clients, and our clients can budget for their bookkeeping costs knowing that they won't have to guess what an hourly invoice will be at the end of each month.

For our clients that we don't have on retainer, we actually rarely invoice. Many of our nonretainer clients are using our remote training, data file setup, or consulting services. For setup services we require full payment prepaid, and for miscellaneous projects (such as entering a backlog of data) we require a 50 percent deposit and the remainder upon completion.

Because our office uses QuickBooks Online, we make ample use of our QuickBooks Merchant Service and our GoPayment accounts. For training and consulting, all remote appointments require a credit card (or e-check) payment before my staff or myself ends the meeting. For workshops or classes, the ability to accept credit card payments via our phones eliminates the risk of receiving bad checks and having to handle large amounts of cash.

Bottom line: Accepting credit cards (and PayPal is always a handy backup if you're ever in a position where you can't take a payment via phone—a button on your website is easy to add and easy to tell your clients to use) and e-checks can save you time and stress by reducing the need to ensure you're being paid on time.

Stacy Kildal, Kildal Services LLC,
www.kildalservices.com, Waterford, MI

Plan for Expenditures

One bonus of providing accounting and bookkeeping services from a home-based office is that not many expenses are involved. However, you can still have some large expenses, which you should plan for to ensure you have adequate cash available to pay them when needed.

Organizations and Memberships

You will have some annual memberships and dues, which can be hundreds of dollars each. For example, you may need to pay dues for the QuickBooks ProAdvisor Program, the chamber of commerce, or other business memberships. If you live in a metro area, usually each city has a chamber of commerce. Joining them all may be cost prohibitive. Many of them will allow you to attend a few events before you join so you can decide whether joining would be a good idea for you. Each group seems to be somewhat unique, and some are more beneficial than others.

Equipment and Other Needs

You need to plan on updating your computer and software every few years so you stay current with technology. This expense will likely be one of your biggest, but your computer and software are the primary "tools" for providing your services. They are important, and you may need to save money so it is available when needed.

You will be wise to set aside money for unexpected expenses or opportunities that may arise. For example, you may have computer problems and need to get it fixed or replaced.

Insurance Needs

You should talk with an insurance agent to ensure you have adequate coverage. You should consider getting errors and omissions (E&O) insurance, which is professional liability insurance that protects you in the event that you make a mistake or are negligent.

Sometimes a client will want to know if you are bonded. If you will have access to or control over client funds or the ability to sign checks, then a surety bond would protect the client from your dishonest acts (i.e., theft). Usually employees are bonded, but you may want or need to be bonded as an independent contractor.

You should also discuss your homeowner's and auto policies with your insurance agent to ensure that you are covered. You may need additional insurance on the homeowner's policy to cover your home office and business assets (furniture, fixtures, equipment, etc.). You may need additional coverage on your auto policy if you use your car for business purposes, too.

If you are a Certified Public Accountant (CPA) who will provide attest services, then you should obtain professional liability insurance. If you provide any audits or reviews, then the cost of the insurance increases significantly and you probably need to budget money for peer review, too. This is one reason why many CPAs do not provide those services.

Estimated Tax Payments

As a new business owner, you may not be familiar with estimated tax payments. When you are an employee, income taxes are withheld from your paycheck and sent to the Internal Revenue Service and your state department of revenue. However, if you are a sole proprietor or limited liability company taxed as a sole proprietor, you need to make estimated tax payments because you do not receive a paycheck.

You will need to submit your estimated tax payments quarterly along with Form 1040-ES and a similar form for your state (i.e., in Missouri it is the MO 1040-ES form). Several rules and exceptions exist, so you should read the details at www.irs.gov to ensure you understand them. If you do not pay your estimated taxes throughout the year, then you may have an underpayment penalty when you file your income taxes.

Retirement Planning

As your business grows, hopefully you will be profitable. When you have sufficient profits and cash flow, then you may want to consider some retirement plans for yourself. Doing this can help you save for retirement and provide some tax-planning opportunities as well. Several options exist, including a SIMPLE (savings incentive match plan for employees) IRA, SEP (simplified employee pension) IRA, individual 401(k), and Keogh plans. The rules and laws change, so when you are interested in retirement planning, you should do your research. You may need to find a trusted investment advisor or tax professional to advise you in this area.

10

Client-Management, Legal, and Ethical Issues

As the owner of your own business, you need to deal with client management and should set up some operating procedures. You can improve your operating efficiency if you develop policies and procedures to follow. Doing this helps ensure that details do not get overlooked and helps you manage the workflow.

In addition, you need to address some legal and ethical issues because you will be dealing with clients' sensitive financial information. If you are a Certified Public Accountant or a tax preparer, then you need to be aware of more stringent requirements and adhere to them in your business.

Client-Acceptance and Retention Policies

One of the reasons why you may be starting your own business is to be your own boss. However, you will quickly learn that you actually have many bosses now—your clients. You will work hard to keep them happy and meet their needs and demands. Doing so will be easy with some clients, and you will enjoy working with them. These are the clients who are organized, respect your time and talents, and pay your fees promptly. There are sample questions to ask potential clients in the sidebar on pages 153-54. You should consider customizing it for questions you would like to ask to determine whether to accept them as a client or not.

However, some clients will be difficult and challenging and try your patience. Some clients will not provide the information you need on a timely basis, or they will fail to include everything you need. However, they still will expect you to get the work completed on time. Some clients may call frequently with questions or request a report and expect immediate attention. A few clients may complain about your high fees and not always pay regularly.

Questions for Potential Clients

[Note: You might not ask these in this exact order]

Your name:

Business name:

Contact info (either e-mail or phone number):

Best time/way to contact you:

What type of product/service do you sell?

What type of entity is your business?
- Sole proprietor
- LLC—single member
- LLC—multiple member
- Partnership
- S corporation
- Corporation
- Nonprofit organization

Is your business a new business or existing business?

For new business:
- When did the business start?

For existing business:
- How were you keeping your accounting records before?
- Are the accounting records in good condition, or do they need work?

Are you new to QuickBooks?

What version of QuickBooks do you have and what year?

- Simple Start

- QuickBooks Pro

- QuickBooks Pro for Mac

- QuickBooks Premier

- QuickBooks Enterprise Solutions

What areas do you need help with?

- Set up the data file?

- Initial training?

- Troubleshooting and fixing problems in the existing data file?

- Training on how to use more features in QB?

- Bookkeeping?

- Payroll?

- Taxes?

- Other—please explain:

Do you prefer someone to come on-site to help you?

Would you like remote assistance?

With remote assistance, you receive an e-mail with a link and instructions, then a request to share control with the Certified ProAdvisor. During the session the ProAdvisor can see and control your computer (just as if he or she were sitting there with you) while talking with you on the phone. When the session ends, the ProAdvisor no longer has access to your computer.

You should consider what type of client you prefer to work with and especially clients you do not want to work with. Also consider if their needs are beyond your level of experience or expertise. For example, if they have not paid or filed their taxes in the past, they may need help with the Internal Revenue Service that requires a CPA or an EA (enrolled agent). You should establish certain criteria up front about the types of clients you will and will not accept. You might want to develop referral relationships for when the need arises.

Similarly, you may find that you no longer want to be associated with clients for one reason or another. Maybe they have quit paying their payroll or sales taxes, or maybe they continue to try to deduct personal expenditures as business expenses. Your reputation is vital to your success, and you might need to fire some clients.

Confidentiality and Security

You need to ensure that you maintain confidentiality and security of your clients' sensitive financial information. You need to ensure security both electronically and physically. Computers and technology were discussed in a prior chapter, but as a reminder you need to ensure that you have adequate security for your computer and for client documents when you send and receive them. You also need to physically secure your computer and client records in your office. A backup plan is important to implement and should include off-site storage.

Engagement Letters

If you are a CPA or an EA, then additional rules and regulations apply to client confidentiality, ethics, security and engagement letters. If you are a CPA, you need to ensure you comply with Statements on Standards for Accounting and Review Standards (SSARS) 19 which requires engagement letters. See sample letters on pages 156–58 and 159–61. Make sure you learn the rules that apply to you based upon your credentials. Following them even if they do not apply to you does not hurt.

Systems and Procedures

Developing systems and procedures helps improve your efficiency and productivity. A variety of methods for working with your clients exists, and the procedures will vary accordingly. You may have clients scan and send you documents; you may work with them online or remotely; or you may still go to their office to do the work. Whichever method works for you, take the time to create some checklists (or use

[NOTE: Download Sample Engagement Letters from Intuit here: http://accountant.intuit.com/ practice_resources/articles/engagementletters.aspx]

<<Client Name>>
<<Company Name>>
<<123 Anywhere Drive>>
<<Anytown, ST 45678>>

Dear <<Client Name>>:

We appreciate the opportunity of providing QuickBooks® accounting setup services to **<<Company Name>>.** To ensure a complete understanding between us, this letter will describe the scope and limitations of the services we will provide for you. **<<Employee Name>>** will be the contact person for this engagement.

What We'll Do
We will create a QuickBooks file for **<<Company Name>>** with transactions that begin on **<<December 31, 2011 (Effective Date)>>.** If needed, we will install the QuickBooks software on the machines you specify. We will record the beginning account balances from a balance sheet you provide. We will set up your QuickBooks preferences and user IDs to reflect your current accounting requirements. We will enter company, customer, vendor, and employee data from information you provide us. We will enter sales items and sales tax information based on information you provide us. If applicable, we will enter inventory items and quantities on hand as provided by you. Also, we will enter payroll items and taxes. We will enter all accounting transactions and reconcile the bank accounts for **<<January 2012>>.** These will be entered from original documents and ledgers you provide.

What We Won't Do
We will make no attempt to adjust the records to reflect generally accepted accounting principles nor to reflect proper tax record keeping. We will make no audit or other verification of the data you submit. We may provide reports that contain portions of financial information; these reports are for internal management use only. We will not provide any financial statements and will not perform any compilation, review, or audit

of any of the financial information. We do not at any time provide legal services of any type. We have not been requested to discover errors, misrepresentations, fraud, illegal acts, or theft. Therefore, we have not included any procedures designed or intended to discover such acts, and you agree we have no responsibility to do so.

What We Need from You

To complete the QuickBooks setup service, we will need to obtain information on a timely and periodic basis from your company. These items include all the input such as a balance sheet as of the effective date of conversion, check registers, bank statements, customer account information, customer invoices, sales ledgers and receipts, sales tax account information, vendor information, purchase orders and vendor invoices, federal tax ID number, payroll information, employee data, unemployment account information, and any other information that we may require to complete the work of this engagement. These items and any other items that we obtain from you will be based on information provided by you and will be used without any further verification or investigation on our part.

When We'll Do It

This engagement will begin on **<<January 10, 2012>>** and is estimated to end on **<<February 10, 2012>>.** This engagement is made on a time-and-materials, best-efforts basis.

Hardware and Software Warranties

During the course of the engagement, we may recommend a purchase and installation of computer or technological hardware, software, communications, or services by your company. Warranties, to the extent they exist, are provided only by the manufacturer/vendor of those computer products.

Services Outside the Scope of This Letter

You may request that we perform additional services at a future date not contemplated by this engagement letter. If this occurs, we will communicate with you regarding the scope and estimated cost of these additional services. Engagements for additional services will necessitate that we issue a separate engagement letter to reflect the obligations of both parties.

Fees

Our fee for these services will be at **<<$xx>>** per hour, plus any out-of-pocket expenses. Invoices will be rendered monthly and are payable on presentation.

Approvals

We are pleased to have you as a client and hope this will begin a long and pleasant association. Please date and sign a copy of this letter and return it to us to acknowledge your agreement with the terms of this engagement.

Sincerely yours,

<<Your signature>>

Acknowledged:

_____   _____

<<Customer>>   **<<Date>>**

[NOTE: Download sample Engagement Letters from Intuit: http://accountant.intuit.com/ practice_resources/articles/engagementletters.aspx]

<<Date>>

<<Client Name>>
<<Company Name>>
<<123 Anywhere Drive>>
<<Anytown, ST 45678>>

Dear **<<Client Name>>:**

We appreciate the opportunity of providing QuickBooks® accounting services to **<<Company Name>>.** To ensure a complete understanding between us, this letter will describe the scope and limitations of the services we will provide for you. **<<Employee Name>>** will be the contact person for this engagement.

What We'll Do

On a monthly basis we will enter all accounting transactions for **<<Company Name>>** into its QuickBooks company file. This includes checks, deposits, and other transactions affecting the checking account. It also includes estimates, invoices, credit memos, and all customer transactions. It includes vendor transactions: bills, item receipts, checks, credit card charges, and purchase orders. We will perform the bank reconciliation for the checking account. We will also enter adjusting journal entries as necessary, including depreciation.

On a semimonthly basis we will prepare payroll for your employees. We will prepare and phone in the accrued payroll liabilities payment using EFTPS. On a quarterly basis we will prepare the federal unemployment tax deposit, and we will prepare and file the federal payroll tax return and state unemployment return. On an annual basis we will prepare the federal unemployment tax return, employee W-2s, W-3 transmittal, and vendor 1099s.

We will set up new customers, employees, and vendors on an as-needed basis. All of the above transactions will be entered from original documents and ledgers you provide.

What We Won't Do

We will make no attempt to adjust the records to reflect generally accepted accounting principles nor to reflect proper tax record keeping. We will make no audit or other verification of the data you submit. We may provide reports that contain portions of financial information; these reports are for internal management use only. We will not provide any financial statements and will not perform any compilation, review, or audit of any of the financial information. We do not at any time provide legal services of any type. We have not been requested to discover errors, misrepresentations, fraud, illegal acts, or theft. Therefore, we have not included any procedures designed or intended to discover such acts, and you agree we have no responsibility to do so.

What We Need from You

To perform our services, we will need to obtain information on a timely and periodic basis from your company. These items include all the input such as check registers, bank statements, customer account information, customer invoices, sales ledgers and receipts, sales tax account information, vendor information, purchase orders and vendor invoices, federal tax ID number, payroll information, employee data, unemployment account information, and any other information that we may require to complete the work of this engagement. These items and any other items that we obtain from you will be based on information provided by you and will be used without any further verification or investigation on our part.

When We'll Do It

This engagement will begin on **<<January 10, 2012>>** and will continue on an as-needed basis or until either party terminates the agreement. This engagement is made on a time-and-materials, best-efforts basis.

Hardware and Software Warranties

During the course of the engagement, we may recommend a purchase and installation of computer or technological hardware, software, communications, or services by your company. Warranties, to the extent they exist, are provided only by the manufacturer/vendor of those computer products.

Services Outside the Scope of This Letter

You may request that we perform additional services at a future date not contemplated by this engagement letter. If this occurs, we will communicate with you regarding the scope and estimated cost of these additional services. Engagements for additional services will necessitate that we issue a separate engagement letter to reflect the obligations of both parties.

Fees

Our fee for these services will be at **<<$xx>>** per hour, plus any out-of-pocket expenses. Invoices will be rendered monthly and are payable on presentation.

Approvals

We are pleased to have you as a client and hope this will begin a long and pleasant association. Please date and sign a copy of this letter and return it to us to acknowledge your agreement with the terms of this engagement.

Sincerely yours,

<<Your signature>>

Acknowledged:

_____   _____

<<Customer>>   **<<Date>>**

Google to find some) for your monthly bookkeeping, QuickBooks setup and training, payroll services, or tax preparation. On pages 164–68 you will find a checklist to help with new QuickBooks clients and a session form to document the work performed.

Also in the appendices the article by Jay Shah discusses how technology has changed throughout the years and how improvements in technology can be utilized to streamline workflow in the accounting process. The article explains how cloud computing (the software is on servers instead of on the computer desktop, providing anywhere, anytime access) is increasingly common. Many accounting professionals are starting to utilize cloud computing to have virtual businesses. You can do all the accounting and bookkeeping work "in the cloud" and work collaboratively with clients.

If you decide you want to outsource some services, numerous firms provide these services to other bookkeepers and accounting professionals. For example, if you will not provide tax preparation services and would like to outsource them to another firm, doing so is easier than ever. One company that provides outsourcing services is Surebooks.

Records Retention and Document Management

If possible you should have clients store and maintain their original client documents and receipts. You do not want to assume the risk nor provide the storage space for original documents. With scanners you can scan the documents in and store them electronically on your computer, on an external hard disk, or on an online service. Scanning and storing are increasingly common, especially because many receipts are no longer readable within a relatively short period of time. Simply filing receipts which would no longer be readable would not be helpful during an audit, so scanning and saving documents to PDF format are a great solution.

Several document-management systems and programs are available to help you store and retrieve documents electronically. You can file the documents in folders electronically just like you would physically file documents in file cabinets. Some document-management programs integrate with QuickBooks, and Intuit offers an "attached document" feature as well. This feature allows you to attach documents (receipts, images, contracts, etc.) to transactions, lists, or other items in QuickBooks. This integration helps you efficiently find and manage documents.

If you are maintaining client files and records, you should adhere to the Internal Revenue Service guidelines. Visit the website www.irs.gov/businesses/small/article/0,,id=98513,00.html for more information. The Massachusetts Society of

Certified Public Accountants has a helpful resource, *The Record Retention Guide*. It covers not only financial information and documents but also other documents. It can be downloaded from www.cpa.net/resources/retengde.pdf to keep as a resource.

State Boards of Accountancy and Regulations for Tax Professionals

Special rules apply to accountants and tax preparers. In certain states (such as Texas), you cannot call yourself an accountant unless you are a Certified Public Accountant. I have heard of people who had to change their business name or their website to remove the reference to "accountant" or "accounting" in order to comply with the rules in their state. Go to your state board of accountancy website to see what the rules are in your state or call the state to ensure you are in compliance.

The rules and regulations for tax preparers continue to get stricter and more difficult to comply with. *Circular 230* from the Internal Revenue Service and the Treasury Department has been around for a number of years to "promote ethical practice by tax professionals." In addition, if you provide tax preparation services or even prepare payroll tax returns for clients, make sure you get a preparer tax identification number (PTIN) and comply with the rules and regulations just recently enacted. You need to be proactive in monitoring new rules and regulations and keep abreast of changes that may apply to you. Subscribe to the IRS or other newsletters or organizations to stay informed.

QuickBooks New Client Setup Checklist

*[NOTE: This can be downloaded from Intuit here: accountant.intuit.com/practice_
resources/articles/practice_development/downloads/qbsetup_engagement_
checklist.doc]*

Engagement: _____

Practitioner: _____

Date or Dates of Completion: _____

Make a check mark (✓) by the number for each item as it is completed.

New Client Info

_____ 1. Collect company information from new client. Include company name, address, phone, e-mail, website, type of entity,
fiscal year start month, tax year start month, and tax ID.

_____ 2. Determine if client will use payroll, inventory, and jobs
features in QuickBooks.

Technology Checkup

_____ 1. Determine if client has sufficient hardware and bandwidth to
run QuickBooks. If not, recommend purchase or upgrade.

_____ 2. Determine if client has the correct version of QuickBooks
to best meet the business needs. If not, recommend purchase
or upgrade.

_____ 3. Install any necessary upgrades to hardware and software
before proceeding. Include maintenance releases from the
Internet after new QuickBooks installation.

Start-Up, Preferences, Opening Balances, and Backup Step

_____ 1. Enter the new client info into the company info of a new file in QuickBooks.

_____ 2. Determine the reporting basis of cash or accrual.

_____ 3. Set up the QuickBooks company preferences.

_____ 4. Set up the chart of accounts including subaccounts.

_____ 5. Determine the QuickBooks start date.

_____ 6. Collect from the client: trial balance as of the start date, bank reconciliations, detail for each of the account balances on the trial balance.

_____ 7. Enter the opening trial balance detail in QuickBooks.

_____ 8. Set up the budget if the client desires.

_____ 9. Determine a backup procedure with the client to be used on an ongoing basis. Include media, frequency, and off-site storage details.

Users

_____ 1. Set up QuickBooks users and install their access settings. Include name, user name, password, areas of access, and access level.

Set Up Lists

_____ 1. Determine if classes are to be used (for department break-down, etc.) and set them up.

_____ 2. Determine which customer and vendor profile lists are to be used and set them up: customer type, vendor type, payment method, terms, ship type, sales rep, and customer message.

_____ 3. Collect the customer information and set up the customer list. Include name, address, phone, fax, e-mail, contact, terms, ship-ping info, sales tax, payment info, credit info, custom fields, and notes.

_____ 4. If the client wants to use jobs, set up jobs and job types. Include name, status, description, and pertinent dates.

_____ 5. Collect the vendor information and set up the vendor list. Include name, address, phone, fax, e-mail, contact, account number, type, terms, 1099 eligibility, custom fields, and notes.

_____ 6. Set up any names that go in the Other Names list.

Set Up Products and Services

_____ 1. Determine the sales tax requirements of the client and set up the sales tax items.

_____ 2. Determine the services and products that are for sale by the client and set them up as items. Do the same for items that are purchased for resale. Determine the correct item type and include descriptions, prices, reorder point if applicable, units of measure, and tax status.

_____ 3. If the client has inventory, enter the quantities. Tie to trial balance.

Set Up Payroll

_____ 1. Determine what payroll service will be used.

_____ 2. Collect payroll tax, payroll tax vendors, salary and wage information, and reimbursement and benefit deduction information and set up payroll items.

_____ 3. Collect employee information and set up employees. Include name, Social Security number, address, wages, additions, deductions, tax details, sick and vacation details, direct deposit, and start date.

_____ 4. If necessary, set up employees' year-to-date payroll figures.

Customizing Features: Forms, Templates, Reports, and Reminders

_____ 1. Order any preprinted forms that the client needs, such as checks, W-2s, invoices, statements, and the like.

_____ 2. Modify templates in the client's desired format. Include invoices, credit memos, estimates, sales receipts, statements, and purchase orders.

_____ 3. Create any form letters to be sent to customers, vendors, employees, or other names in QuickBooks.

_____ 4. Modify any settings, fonts, and margins necessary on printed forms (using printer setup in the file menu).

_____ 5. Memorize reports desired by client.

_____ 6. Set up and customize reminders to the client's wishes.

_____ 7. Set up to do list, if needed.

_____ 8. Modify user preferences as desired. Customize icon bar, desktop view.

Transactions

_____ 1. Enter client transactions since the start date. Include estimates, invoices, credit memos, sales orders, sales receipts, checks, bills, purchase orders, deposits, credit card charges, time data, payroll checks, payroll liability payments, and journal entries.

_____ 2. Complete any bank reconciliations during the period.

_____ 3. Memorize recurring transactions.

_____ 4. Perform a backup of the work entered so far.

Additional Features

_____ 1. Determine if client needs these additional services and subscribe them: online banking, merchant credit card services, credit check services, shipping, and remote access.

Your Name

Installation, Account Setup, Training, Troubleshooting

123 Main St.
Anytown, MO 12345
Office: (888) 123-4567
Cell: (999) 876-4321

Next Appointment: _____

Session Report

Client: _____

Date: _____

Hours From: _____
Hours To: _____
Hours Total: _____

Items Covered Today

_____
_____
_____
_____
_____
_____

Items to Cover Next Session

_____
_____
_____
_____
_____
_____

Client Homework

_____
_____
_____
_____
_____
_____

ProAdvisor Homework

_____
_____
_____
_____
_____
_____

_____
Client

_____
Your Business, LLC
Your Name
Certified ProAdvisor (or other)

1. Copy to Client   2. Copy to File
E-mail: ❑ Entered: _____

Appendix A: Resources

Business Counseling and Resources

www.sba.gov (specifically the Small Business Development Center)

www.score.org (Service Corps of Retired Executives)

Business Plans

www.bplans.com/accounting_and_bookkeeping_business_plan/
executive_summary_fc.cfm

www.sba.gov/smallbusinessplanner/plan/writeabusinessplan/
index.html

www.score.org/template_gallery.html

Document-Retention Resources

www.cpa.net/resources/retengde.pdf

www.irs.gov/businesses/small/article/0,,id=98513,00.html

Licensing

www.sba.gov/hotlist/license.html (list of state licensing bureaus)

Legal

www.legalzoom.com (online document-filing service to form a
corporation or LLC)

www.mycorporation.com (online document-filing service to form a corporation or LLC)

www.nolo.com (Nolo has books and resources to help form a business entity.)

Marketing

www.hubspot.com (resource for social media marketing, free webinars, etc.)

http://Intuit.99designs.com (logo or other graphics work)

www.overnightprints.com (business cards, postcards, and other printing needs)

www.vistaprint.com (business cards, postcards, and other printing needs)

Organizations and Certifications

http://proadvisor.intuit.com (QuickBooks ProAdvisor program & certification)

www.aicpa.org (American Institute of Certified Public Accountants)

www.aipb.org/ (American Institute of Professional Bookkeepers)

www.americanpayroll.org/certification/ (American Payroll Association)

www.nacpb.org (National Association of Certified Professional Bookkeepers)

www.naea.org (National Association of Enrolled Agents)

www.nationaladvisornetwork.com (National Advisor Network—Intuit advisors, including QuickBooks)

www.natptax.com (National Association of Tax Professionals)

www.nsacct.org (National Society of Accountants)

www.pennfoster.edu (Penn Foster—bookkeeping education)

www.sleeter.com (Sleeter Group—experts in accounting software, including QuickBooks)

www.universalaccounting.com (Universal Accounting)

Social Media and Social Networking

http://community.intuit.com (Intuit community forums)

www.facebook.com

www.facebook.com/LongforSuccess (my Facebook page for my business)

www.Linkedin.com

www.linkedin.com/groupRegistration?gid=157449 (Successful QuickBooks Consultants/Consulting —Accounting & Bookkeeping—Long for Success group)

www.twitter.com

www.twitter.com/longforsuccess (my business Twitter account)

www.twitter.com/michellelongcpa (my Twitter account)

Social Media Tools

http://ping.fm

www.hootesuite.com

www.socialooph.com

URL Shortening

http://bit.ly

http://tinyurl.com

Website Hosting, Design, and Resources

www.godaddy.com (GoDaddy)

www.google.com/addurl/?continue=/addurl (submit your website to Google)

www.hubspot.com (resource for social media marketing, free webinars, etc.)

www.intuit.com/website-building-software/ (Intuit websites)

www.officelive.com/free-Website?xid=c2logo (Microsoft Office Live—free website and hosting)

www.Websitegrader.com (analyze your website)

www.Websites4accountants.com (comparison of full-service website providers)

Client Portals

www.leapfile.com

www.sharefile.com

www.tweetdeck.com

Appendix B:
Overview of the Evolution of Bookkeeping to Web-Based, Saas Accounting Applications

In the accounting and bookkeeping industry, the topic of cloud computing is becoming more prevalent. Increasingly bookkeepers are working with clients using online mechanisms for transferring source documents, sending files, or accessing computers remotely. Many bookkeepers have virtual businesses and have only remote clients across the country. The Internet has opened the doors of opportunity and resulted in new programs, services, and options to enhance our productivity and efficiency when working with clients.

The following article by Jay Shah (see bio at the end) reviews the history and evolution of the accounting industry and the challenges faced by bookkeepers and accountants. It introduces cloud computing, hosted programs, and web-based, SaaS accounting applications.

Brief History of Bookkeeping

The fundamentals of double-entry accounting have remained the same from Luca Pacioli's time, but the tools used to keep the books have evolved over time. Paper, pencil, and ledgers lasted for centuries. Then corporations used main frame computers in the late 1960s. In the early 1980s we saw the IBM P.C. and spreadsheet programs such as Visicalc, which encouraged accounting professionals to begin using P.C.s. Next was the development of various accounting and tax software programs.

Software "automated" double-entry bookkeeping and virtually eliminated the paper journals and ledgers. This advance made the bookkeeping process smoother with fewer chances of calculation errors or postings to the wrong column or ledger that were inherent in the paper-and-pencil environment.

Even in the new environment, drastic changes occurred over the years (and we all went kicking and screaming—change is hard). First we had single-tasking DOS—command line and keyboard-driven access. This was followed by multitasking and mouse-driven graphical access of Windows. Many felt that DOS was faster, and they were not willing to move to Windows. But that soon changed as many found Windows to be better.

In the 1990s Intuit expanded its successful Quicken personal finance (check book writer) software and introduced QuickBooks accounting software for small business. Fairly quickly QuickBooks became the leader in small business accounting software.

However, accounting programs for small businesses also created a whole new opportunity for independent bookkeepers and accountants to assist small business owners. Most small business owners do not know accounting fundamentals. They were using powerful accounting software and making errors—a simple example is when the purchase of a car would show up as an expense instead of as an asset.

Along with errors from the users themselves, desktop accounting software (as much as it automated the double-entry system and eliminated the paper-and-pencil approach) also created certain inefficiencies in the bookkeeping process. Often the bookkeeper has to adapt to work with the client based on which program the client has and which version he is using. This situation results in several inefficiencies, such as:

- Every year a new version of the program (i.e. Quickbooks), with new functionality and enhancements, comes along, and after a file is upgraded to the new version, it cannot be opened by older versions of the program. This situation is not a problem if the bookkeeper is the only one working in the file, and it is not being used by the client. However, when the client, too, is using the file (to enter transactions, generate reports, etc.), then the bookkeeper must keep track of which version of the program the client is using. Generally the client does not upgrade his program every year, so the bookkeeper must not upgrade the file to a newer version, or else the client cannot open it anymore.
- If the client or his employees enter transactions and work in the file, then the file needs to be sent back and forth between the client and the bookkeeper. This process is inefficient and cumbersome.
- In general, one master file exists, so, while the bookkeeper is working with the file, neither the client nor the employees can be entering transactions at the same time. This is another area of inefficiency.

- Often the size of the file becomes too large to send via normal e-mail.
- Sometimes these problems and inefficiencies require the bookkeeper to travel to the client's office to do the work. The travel time is nonproductive time for the bookkeeper and may result in additional fees to the client.
- These limitations also limit the market for potential clients to those clients who are within short driving distance, and, if the client moves, then you lose the client.
- In the past few years, using remote access to log into clients' computers remotely allows bookkeepers to avoid issues with sharing the file and the travel time to clients' offices.
- However, if the bookkeeper is working in a client's file remotely, then the client cannot use the computer at the same time. Often the bookkeeper has to do the work at odd hours.
- Other considerations include having proper security measures like a fire-wall, antivirus, and malware software that would not erase the work file.
- Plus, multiple backups (including one off-site) must be made to protect against a disaster or equipment failure.

People had no alternative to these inherent inefficiencies in the desktop environment, and we tolerated and kept finding ways to deal with them as effectively as possible. But this situation affected the productivity and profitability of bookkeepers and accountants.

The Internet Creates Opportunities

Although the Internet has been around since the late 1960s in the armed forces and universities, it really came to the commercial age in the 1990s. The Internet leveled the playing field and created many opportunities. Because of the Internet, a part-time bookkeeper working from the kitchen table can build her business without geographic limitations. Potential clients do not need to see the physical office of the bookkeeper, but they can learn everything from the bookkeeper's website. Web 1.0 was born!

Today the software can reside on commercial server farms that are accessible from anywhere and at anytime. One of the early examples of this arrangement was Hotmail. Hotmail is e-mail software hosted on a remote server that can be accessed anytime and from anywhere. An office e-mail server is not needed. This arrangement allows the masses to have access to e-mail communication without the cost of a mail server. Just a computer and even a dial-up connection to the Internet are enough to communicate with anyone around the world who has the same environment of a computer and Internet access.

Cloud Computing

The Internet was called a "cloud" because it was always shown as a cloud in network diagrams because no one really owns the Internet as a whole. This new environment—the software is installed on a remote computer managed by someone else and can be accessed through the cloud (i.e., the Internet)—came to be known as "cloud computing."

This development has started to change the desktop paradigm (programs installed on your computer) and some of the inefficiencies in the bookkeeping process discussed above. Naturally accounting desktop software went onto these servers as hosted programs. This arrangement provides both the bookkeeper and the client access from anywhere at anytime. This advance enables an even greater market reach beyond the local area.

Hosted programs allow access from anywhere at anytime and minimize files going back and forth between the accountant and client. However, there are two basic issues: (1) The Internet is slow for some users, and (2) its availability is not universal. In addition, some of the other inefficiencies listed above remain (different versions of a program and backward compatibility, client-generated errors, etc.) because this is still the same desktop software. The only difference is that it is now housed on a remote computer. Thus, some of the problems of the desktop environment may still exist.

Web 2.0, SaaS, and Web-Based Computing

In the late 1990s and early in the year 2000, a whole new generation of software was designed for the web environment. These programs were designed from the ground up as opposed to just taking desktop software and hosting it on a server.

This new paradigm of software allowed true collaboration between people in real time. The whole collaborative aspect of the Internet came to be known as "web 2.0." Facebook, Twitter, LinkedIn, etc. are just a few examples of this aspect.

Some established vendors of desktop accounting software (that was targeted for accounting professionals as opposed to end users) adopted this new paradigm of collaboration. They sought to eliminate inefficiencies in the bookkeeping process in the desktop environment. One of these vendors was MicroVision. It restructured and created a new company called "AccountantsWorld" to offer web 2.0-based collaborative accounting solutions. These types of solutions are called "SaaS" (software as a service), and this new computing environment came to be known as "web-based computing" (versus cloud computing).

Other companies, such as NetSuite, existed, but they targeted large enterprises and large CPA firms as opposed to sole practitioners and small accounting firms. In 2000, Intuit created an online version of QuickBooks for small businesses that need access from anywhere at anytime called QuickBooks Online Edition. AccountantsWorld created Accounting Relief (a SaaS solution) when it gutted the entire desktop-based bookkeeping process to eliminate inefficiencies and create a seamless collaborative accounting process that saves time and virtually eliminates client-generated errors.

In the web 2.0 paradigm, software resides on the server, and everyone gets the same set/subset of the functionality, eliminating all versions and updates. When the functionality is updated, nothing has to be downloaded and installed for the update. The update is made on the software at the server—just one place—and everyone now has the latest version.

No problem of backward compatibility of files exists because everyone has the same version. Of course, having access from anywhere at anytime eliminates the need for travel. It also eliminates any cost of remote access to the client's computer and the need to work odd hours when using remote access. And the need to send files back and forth no longer exists.

Example of the Benefits of a Web 2.0/SaaS Program

The following example illustrates how a bookkeeper would work with clients using a web 2.0 or SaaS program and the benefits and security.

More Efficient Workflow Process

This diagram illustrates the typical twelve steps in the bookkeeping process when you are working with a client in a desktop environment (courtesy of Dr. Chandra Bhansali, president of AccountantsWorld).

Workflow in Desktop Accounting

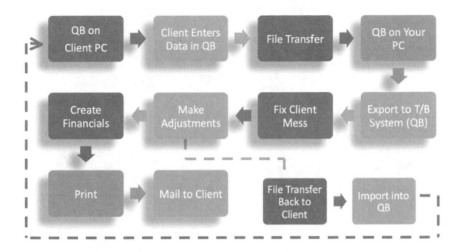

Using a collaborative, web 2.0-based accounting service such as Accounting Relief from AccountantsWorld eliminates eight of the twelve steps, as shown below.

Web-Based Accounting Eliminates Steps

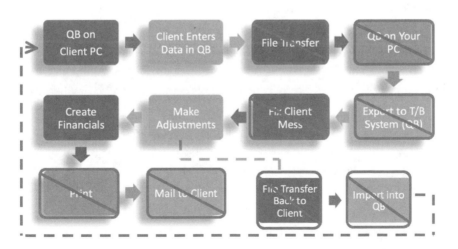

As a result, the web-based accounting service is now a streamlined process, as shown below.

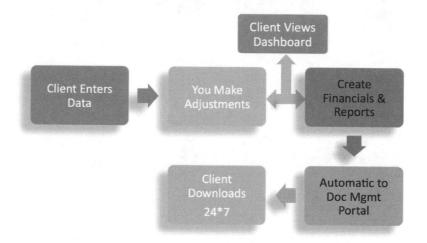

Workflow in Web-Based Accounting

Client Enters Data → You Make Adjustments → Create Financials & Reports → Client Views Dashboard

Create Financials & Reports → Automatic to Doc Mgmt Portal → Client Downloads 24*7

This streamlined process accomplishes the same work in less time, making the bookkeeper and client more productive. They can work independently and still have synchronized files available anytime and from anywhere. With a more efficient workflow and extra time, the bookkeeper can work on more clients and offer value-added services that were not possible before due to the time constraints.

Minimize Client Errors—Control Access

This simplification of the process saves time, but how can you minimize client-generated errors in a web 2.0 environment? These errors usually occur when clients lack accounting fundamentals (which you should not expect from clients) and have too much access to all the functionality of the software (when they may need just to update a customer or vendor, enter a check or invoice). If clients (or an employee) have the knowledge, then you can give them a higher level of access to other functions as deemed appropriate. This kind of selective user access can minimize or eliminate client errors by controlling the areas of access.

SaaS services such as Accounting Relief allow you to control client access at a granular level by creating many "versions" of the application geared specifically to clients' capabilities and no more. You have no reason to give clients access to a chart of accounts (COA) when they do not have solid accounting fundamentals.

This controlled access, combined with the ability to work collaboratively with the client, changes the whole paradigm of the current desktop accounting process.

Look below at the various levels (and subsets) of access you can configure in Accounting Relief. These settings allow you to control the activities you want your client to perform when using Accounting Relief.

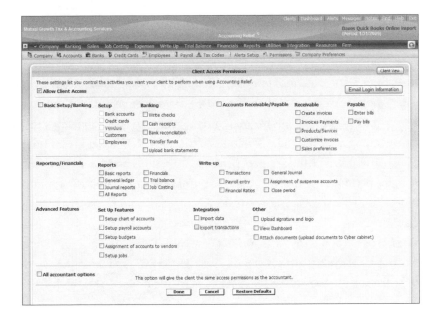

Security Concerns

One issue that pops up frequently is that of security and privacy in an Internet-based environment. Some accountants, bookkeepers, and clients do not think twice about shopping online with their credit card or performing online banking, yet they hesitate with their accounting data. However, all SaaS applications use SSL access. This means you have to type the web address as "https" and not "http," which provides a minimum of 128-bit encryptions (like banks use) or higher.

In reality, a SaaS environment has far better security and safety than do the computers of most small businesses. Rarely you will come across someone using an encrypted hard drive on his computer. Many people do not run the right antivirus or malware software. Some people even use a service such as torrent and do unsafe surfing that results in a virus. Some viruses not only wipe out the entire hard drive but also install stealth key-logger software that captures (and sends to the hacker) all of your keyboard strokes, including your login, password, and credit card information. In fact, relatively few people use strong passwords and instead use the same password for all their online services (or, worse, write that password on a Post-it Note and stick it on the monitor). Thus, a single compromised password will provide hackers with access to everything. Plus, how many clients actually take multiple levels of backup of data on an external hard drive or online vaults and/or take disk images?

True commercial SaaS providers use an industrial-grade data center with duplicate servers on different electric power grids, extra power generators and cooling, and retina and fingerprint scans to enter the locked cage in which the server resides. They have strong antivirus and malware software with no Internet access (to bring in a virus) other than for their remote backup data centers and for user access. Not only do they perform local backups, but also the backups are stored off-site so in the event of natural disaster they can be restored quickly on another server and can be up in a short time.

All of these features of SaaS not only provide strong physical and software security but also have sophisticated data integrity software so that in the event of a crash the backup can be restored and data integrity maintained. How many of these precautions are available, and at what cost, in a desktop environment?

What does all this mean to you? Well, other than death and taxes, nothing is constant. Things change. A good and properly implemented change can result in new efficiencies to the entire bookkeeping process, increasing revenues, profitability, and client retention.

Conclusion

This gives you just a taste of the pending changes in the way you do bookkeeping and hopefully will encourage you to start testing the water by putting your toes into this new paradigm. I should point out that as with any change, resistance will come not only from accountants and bookkeepers but also from clients. For a while you possibly will maintain a dual environment of desktop and web-based accounting SaaS applications.

Now, with much greater Internet access and usage, you will find a new set of clients whose members are not afraid or are even willing to use the web-based approach. Put them on SaaS programs and slowly educate current clients to move away from the desktop environment. Just as DOS went away and as support for earlier versions of desktop software has gone away, the desktop environment will go away in upcoming years. You can handhold these clients to migrate to the new environment. They (and you) will be highly appreciative of this change.

Happy cloud and web accounting!

■　　　　　■　　　　　■

The author **Jay Shah** is happily married with two grown children and lives with his lovely wife Anu in Old Bridge, NJ, and remains active even after two retirements.

He has several graduate degrees in physics and computer science. He taught in high school, two-year community college, and four-year college as well as at university for twelve years before switching to Illinois Bell and Bell Labs under AT&T and Lucent. Before he retired he was director of Lucent's worldwide data, voice, and video network architecture, design, and product management. He led the network split between AT&T and Lucent, one of the largest IP networks behind the U.S. government, and retired in 2000 after twenty years.

After he retired from Lucent he was invited by Dr. Bhansali to help form AccountantsWorld and offer web-based accounting services for accountants only. He retired from AccountantsWorld in 2006. Now he enjoys retirement with leisure and spiritual enrichment and helps other business owners with process, management, and technology issues. Visit him at his website, www.jaysonlineoffice.com.

Appendix C: Useful Forms

You will need to complete and file various forms with your state (such as Articles of Incorporation, Articles of Formation, Registration of Fictitious Name), depending on which type of business entity you select. In many states the Secretary of State's website will provide information about which forms are required for each type of entity, along with the costs. Some states provide the required documents as PDF forms, which you can complete and file online (or print for your attorney to review). For example, see the following forms from the Missouri Secretary of State's website.

If your state does not provide the forms online, then you have other options. Online companies (MyCorporation, LegalZoom, etc.) help you complete and file the forms with your state. You can use Google to find sample forms that you need. Finally, the public library usually has books, such as *How to Form Your Own LLC* with a CD of sample forms. (Or you could order the book online at www.nolo.com.) After you prepare the required documents, you may wish to have your attorney review them.

After you have registered your business with the state, the next step is to obtain an employer identification number (EIN), which may be called a "tax ID number," from the Internal Revenue Service. Go to www.irs.gov to fill out the EIN application (SS-4) and obtain an EIN for your business. You need to indicate the business name and type of entity, so you cannot do this until those steps have been completed. Please see Form SS-4—Application for Employer ID Number included in this appendix.

ROBIN CARNAHAN
SECRETARY OF STATE
STATE OF MISSOURI

JAMES C. KIRKPATRICK
STATE INFORMATION CENTER
(573) 751-4936

CORPORATIONS
(573) 751-4153

Limited Liability Company Instruction Sheet

Here is information we hope you will find useful in considering the organization of a Missouri Liability Company.

1. The following should be considered when determining the name of the limited liability company:

    A. The name must be distinguishable from the name of a domestic limited liability company currently in existence, any foreign limited liability company which is qualified and in good standing, any corporation, limited partnership, limited liability partnership, limited liability limited partnership, or a name which is currently reserved.

    B. The limited liability company name may not be one that might imply that the company is a government agency.

    C. The words corporation, incorporated, limited partnership, L.P. or Ltd., or an abbreviation of one of such words, may not be used in the name.

    D. Name Check. Before drafting articles of organization it is imperative that you check with this office concerning the availability of the desired name. This may be done by mail or telephone by calling either (573) 751-4153 or (866) 223-6535 (toll-free). You may also select the Online Business Services business entity search at *www.sos.mo.gov*. Even though a name may have been checked with us for availability, any documents such as checks, letterhead, seals or certificates ordered prior to organization are purchased at your own risk. We recommend that nothing be printed until the company is organized by this office and you have received your certificate of organization.

    E. Reservation of name. If you wish, you may reserve a corporate name in advance. You may request a reservation with either a letter or form from this office. A name may be reserved for 60 days, and a fee of $25.00 must accompany a reservation of a name. The name may not be reserved for more than 180 days.

2. The article listing the purpose or purposes should include at least one sentence which defines the specific purpose for which the company is organized (for example, what it will do to make a profit). You may also include, if desired, a purpose statement such as "and all other legal acts permitted limited liability companies."

3. The limited liability company must have a registered agent and office **in** Missouri. The registered agent may be an individual who is a resident of this State, or a domestic corporation or foreign corporation authorized to do business in this State. The registered agent's business office address must be identical to the address of the registered office.

PO BOX 778 • JEFFERSON CITY, MISSOURI • 65102
www.sos.mo.gov

4. The articles of organization must state who will manage the company. A limited liability company is managed by its members or by a manager or managers. Either option is permissible, though the choice of management structure may have legal ramifications concerning the liability of the members and/or managers. Managers are not required by law to be members of the limited liability company.

5. The articles of organization must state the event by which the limited liability company is to dissolve. The event may state that the company will dissolve upon the occurrence of a specific event; a set number of years or upon reaching a specific date in the future; or the duration may be perpetual, meaning there is no expiration.

6. A limited liability company must have at least one organizer, which is the person or persons who sign the articles or organization. A limited liability company may have more than one organizer. Organizers do not have to be members or owners of the company, nor do they have to be managers of the company. If none of the registered agent, members or managers (if any) can be located, service of process for a civil lawsuit may be served on an organizer.

Feel free to call our office toll-free at (866) 223-6535 with any questions you may have concerning these instructions.

Sincerely,

Robin Carnahan
Secretary of State

State of Missouri

Robin Carnahan, Secretary of State

Corporations Division
PO Box 778 / 600 W. Main St., Rm. 322
Jefferson City. MO 65102

Articles of Organization
(Submit with filing fee of $105.00)

1. The name of the limited liability company is

   _____

   (Must include "Limited Liability Company," "Limited Company," "LC," "L.C.," "L.L.C.," or "LLC")

2. The purpose(s) for which the limited liability company is organized: _____

   _____

3. The name and address of the limited liability company's registered agent in Missouri is:

   _____

   Name   Street Address: May not use PO Box unless street address also provided   City/State/Zip

4. The management of the limited liability company is vested in: ☐ managers   ☐ members   (check one)

5. The events, if any, on which the limited liability company is to dissolve or the number of years the limited liability company is to

   continue, which may be any number or perpetual: _____

   _____

   (The answer to this question could cause possible tax consequences. you may wish to consult with your attorney or accountant)

6. The name(s) and street address(es) of each organizer (PO box may only be used in addition to a physical street address):
   (Organizer(s) are not required to be member(s), manager(s) or owner(s)

   _____

   _____

   _____

7. The effective date of this document is the date it is filed by the Secretary of State of Missouri unless a future date is otherwise

   indicated: _____

   (Date may not be more than 90 days after the filing date in this office)

(Please see next page)

Name and address to return filed document:

Name: _____

Address: _____

City, State, and Zip Code: _____

LLC-1 (11/2008)

In Affirmation thereof, the facts stated above are true and correct:
(The undersigned understands that false statements made in this filing are subject to the penalties provided under Section 575.040, RSMo)
All organizers must sign:

_____   _____   _____
Organizer Signature   Printed Name   Date

_____   _____   _____
Organizer Signature   Printed Name   Date

_____   _____   _____
Organizer Signature   Printed Name   Date

State of Missouri
Robin Carnahan, Secretary of State

Corporations Division
PO Box 2050 / 600 W. Main St., Rm. 322
Jefferson City, MO 65102

Registration of Fictitious Name
(Submit with filing fee of $7.00)
(Must be typed or printed)

This information is for the use of the public and gives no protection to the name being registered. There is no provision in this Chapter to keep another person or business entity from adopting and using the same name. The fictitious name registration expires 5 years from the filing date. (Chapter 417, RSMo)

Please check one box:

☐ New Registration ☐ Renewal X_____ ☐ Amendment X_____ ☐ Correction X_____
                         Charter number   Charter number   Charter number

The undersigned is doing business under the following name and at the following address:

Business name to be registered: _____

Business Address: _____
                    (PO Box may only be used in addition to a physical street address)

City, State and Zip Code: _____

Owner Information:

If a business entity is an owner, indicate business name and percentage owned. If all parties are jointly and severally liable, percentage of ownership need not be listed. Please attach a separate page for more than three owners. The parties having an interest in the business, and the percentage they own are:

Name of Owners, Individual or Business Entity	Charter # Required If Business Entity	Street and Number	City and State	Zip Code	If Listed, Percentage of Ownership Must Equal 100%

All owners must affirm by signing below

In Affirmation thereof, the facts stated above are true and correct:

(The undersigned understands that false statements made in this filing are subject to the penalties of a false declaration under Section 575.060 RSMo)

_____   _____   _____
Owner's Signature or Authorized Signature of Business Entity   *Printed Name*   *Date*

_____   _____   _____
Owner's Signature or Authorized Signature of Business Entity   *Printed Name*   *Date*

_____   _____   _____
Owner's Signature or Authorized Signature of Business Entity   *Printed Name*   *Date*

Name and address to return filed document:

Name: _____

Address: _____

City, State, and Zip Code: _____

Corp. 56 (09/2010)

Form **SS-4**
(Rev. January 2010)
Department of the Treasury
Internal Revenue Service

Application for Employer Identification Number

(For use by employers, corporations, partnerships, trusts, estates, churches, government agencies, Indian tribal entities, certain individuals, and others.)

▶ See separate instructions for each line. ▶ Keep a copy for your records.

OMB No. 1545-0003

EIN

Type or print clearly.

1	Legal name of entity (or individual) for whom the EIN is being requested

2	Trade name of business (if different from name on line 1)	3	Executor, administrator, trustee, "care of" name

4a	Mailing address (room, apt., suite no. and street, or P.O. box)	5a	Street address (if different) (Do not enter a P.O. box.)
4b	City, state, and ZIP code (if foreign, see instructions)	5b	City, state, and ZIP code (if foreign, see instructions)

6	County and state where principal business is located

7a	Name of responsible party	7b	SSN, ITIN, or EIN

8a Is this application for a limited liability company (LLC) (or a foreign equivalent)? . . . . ☐ Yes ☐ No   **8b** If 8a is "Yes," enter the number of LLC members . . . . ▶

8c If 8a is "Yes," was the LLC organized in the United States? . . . . ☐ Yes ☐ No

9a **Type of entity** (check only one box). **Caution.** If 8a is "Yes," see the instructions for the correct box to check.

☐ Sole proprietor (SSN) _____
☐ Partnership
☐ Corporation (enter form number to be filed) ▶_____
☐ Personal service corporation
☐ Church or church-controlled organization
☐ Other nonprofit organization (specify) ▶_____
☐ Other (specify) ▶

☐ Estate (SSN of decedent) _____
☐ Plan administrator (TIN) _____
☐ Trust (TIN of grantor) _____
☐ National Guard   ☐ State/local government
☐ Farmers' cooperative ☐ Federal government/military
☐ REMIC ☐ Indian tribal governments/enterprises
Group Exemption Number (GEN) if any ▶

9b If a corporation, name the state or foreign country (if applicable) where incorporated

State	Foreign country

10 **Reason for applying** (check only one box)
☐ Started new business (specify type) ▶ _____
☐ Hired employees (Check the box and see line 13.)
☐ Compliance with IRS withholding regulations
☐ Other (specify) ▶

☐ Banking purpose (specify purpose) ▶_____
☐ Changed type of organization (specify new type) ▶_____
☐ Purchased going business
☐ Created a trust (specify type) ▶_____
☐ Created a pension plan (specify type) ▶_____

11 Date business started or acquired (month, day, year). See instructions.

12 Closing month of accounting year

13 Highest number of employees expected in the next 12 months (enter -0- if none).

If no employees expected, skip line 14.

Agricultural	Household	Other

14 If you expect your employment tax liability to be $1,000 or less in a full calendar year **and** want to file Form 944 annually instead of Forms 941 quarterly, check here. (Your employment tax liability generally will be $1,000 or less if you expect to pay $4,000 or less in total wages.) If you do not check this box, you must file Form 941 for every quarter. ☐

15 First date wages or annuities were paid (month, day, year). **Note.** If applicant is a withholding agent, enter date income will first be paid to nonresident alien (month, day, year) . . . . ▶

16 Check **one** box that best describes the principal activity of your business.
☐ Construction ☐ Rental & leasing ☐ Transportation & warehousing ☐ Health care & social assistance ☐ Wholesale-agent/broker
☐ Real estate ☐ Manufacturing ☐ Finance & insurance ☐ Accommodation & food service ☐ Wholesale-other ☐ Retail
☐ Other (specify)

17 Indicate principal line of merchandise sold, specific construction work done, products produced, or services provided.

18 Has the applicant entity shown on line 1 ever applied for and received an EIN? ☐ Yes ☐ No
If "Yes," write previous EIN here ▶

Third Party Designee

Complete this section **only** if you want to authorize the named individual to receive the entity's EIN and answer questions about the completion of this form.

Designee's name	Designee's telephone number (include area code) ( )
Address and ZIP code	Designee's fax number (include area code) ( )

Under penalties of perjury, I declare that I have examined this application, and to the best of my knowledge and belief, it is true, correct, and complete.

Name and title (type or print clearly) ▶

Applicant's telephone number (include area code) ( )

Signature ▶   Date ▶

Applicant's fax number (include area code) ( )

For Privacy Act and Paperwork Reduction Act Notice, see separate instructions.   Cat. No. 16055N   Form **SS-4** (Rev. 1-2010)

Do I Need an EIN?

File Form SS-4 if the applicant entity does not already have an EIN but is required to show an EIN on any return, statement, or other document.[1] See also the separate instructions for each line on Form SS-4.

IF the applicant...	AND...	THEN...
Started a new business	Does not currently have (nor expect to have) employees	Complete lines 1, 2, 4a–8a, 8b–c (if applicable), 9a, 9b (if applicable), and 10–14 and 16–18.
Hired (or will hire) employees, including household employees	Does not already have an EIN	Complete lines 1, 2, 4a–6, 7a–b (if applicable), 8a, 8b–c (if applicable), 9a, 9b (if applicable), 10–18.
Opened a bank account	Needs an EIN for banking purposes only	Complete lines 1–5b, 7a–b (if applicable), 8a, 8b–c (if applicable), 9a, 9b (if applicable), 10, and 18.
Changed type of organization	Either the legal character of the organization or its ownership changed (for example, you incorporate a sole proprietorship or form a partnership)[2]	Complete lines 1–18 (as applicable).
Purchased a going business[3]	Does not already have an EIN	Complete lines 1–18 (as applicable).
Created a trust	The trust is other than a grantor trust or an IRA trust[4]	Complete lines 1–18 (as applicable).
Created a pension plan as a plan administrator[5]	Needs an EIN for reporting purposes	Complete lines 1, 3, 4a–5b, 9a, 10, and 18.
Is a foreign person needing an EIN to comply with IRS withholding regulations	Needs an EIN to complete a Form W-8 (other than Form W-8ECI), avoid withholding on portfolio assets, or claim tax treaty benefits[6]	Complete lines 1–5b, 7a–b (SSN or ITIN optional), 8a, 8b–c (if applicable), 9a, 9b (if applicable), 10, and 18.
Is administering an estate	Needs an EIN to report estate income on Form 1041	Complete lines 1–6, 9a, 10–12, 13–17 (if applicable), and 18.
Is a withholding agent for taxes on non-wage income paid to an alien (i.e., individual, corporation, or partnership, etc.)	Is an agent, broker, fiduciary, manager, tenant, or spouse who is required to file Form 1042, Annual Withholding Tax Return for U.S. Source Income of Foreign Persons	Complete lines 1, 2, 3 (if applicable), 4a–5b, 7a–b (if applicable), 8a, 8b–c (if applicable), 9a, 9b (if applicable), 10, and 18.
Is a state or local agency	Serves as a tax reporting agent for public assistance recipients under Rev. Proc. 80-4, 1980-1 C.B. 581[7]	Complete lines 1, 2, 4a–5b, 9a, 10, and 18.
Is a single-member LLC	Needs an EIN to file Form 8832, Classification Election, for filing employment tax returns and excise tax returns, or for state reporting purposes[8]	Complete lines 1–18 (as applicable).
Is an S corporation	Needs an EIN to file Form 2553, Election by a Small Business Corporation[9]	Complete lines 1–18 (as applicable).

[1] For example, a sole proprietorship or self-employed farmer who establishes a qualified retirement plan, or is required to file excise, employment, alcohol, tobacco, or firearms returns, must have an EIN. A partnership, corporation, REMIC (real estate mortgage investment conduit), nonprofit organization (church, club, etc.), or farmers' cooperative must use an EIN for any tax-related purpose even if the entity does not have employees.

[2] However, do not apply for a new EIN if the existing entity only (a) changed its business name, (b) elected on Form 8832 to change the way it is taxed (or is covered by the default rules), or (c) terminated its partnership status because at least 50% of the total interests in partnership capital and profits were sold or exchanged within a 12-month period. The EIN of the terminated partnership should continue to be used. See Regulations section 301.6109-1(d)(2)(iii).

[3] Do not use the EIN of the prior business unless you became the "owner" of a corporation by acquiring its stock.

[4] However, grantor trusts that do not file using Optional Method 1 and IRA trusts that are required to file Form 990-T, Exempt Organization Business Income Tax Return, must have an EIN. For more information on grantor trusts, see the Instructions for Form 1041.

[5] A plan administrator is the person or group of persons specified as the administrator by the instrument under which the plan is operated.

[6] Entities applying to be a Qualified Intermediary (QI) need a QI-EIN even if they already have an EIN. See Rev. Proc. 2000-12.

[7] See also *Household employer* on page 4 of the instructions. **Note.** State or local agencies may need an EIN for other reasons, for example, hired employees.

[8] See *Disregarded entities* on page 4 of the instructions for details on completing Form SS-4 for an LLC.

[9] An existing corporation that is electing or revoking S corporation status should use its previously-assigned EIN.

Index

types of services to offer, 18–19, 29–30, 57, 102
visualizing your business in the future, 16–18
business entities
and the corporate veil, 66
corporations, 61–64, 66
limited liability companies (LLC), 62, 64
partnerships, 60–61, 62
selection guide, 62–63
sole proprietorships, 60, 62
Business Plan Pro, 24
Business to Consumer (B2C), 131

C

Camtasia Studio, 134–35
Carbonite, 80
Certified Bookkeeper (CB) designation, 93–94
Certified Bookkeeper Survey-2010, 92
Certified Fraud Examiner (CFE), 96
Certified Managerial Accountant (CMA), 96
Certified Payroll Professional (CPP) certification, 96
Certified Payroll Specialist, 94
Certified ProAdvisors, 25–26
Certified Public Accountant (CPA), 96, 151, 155, 168
Certified Public Bookkeeper (CPB), 94–95
Certified Quickbooks Advisor, 94, 144–45
Christiansen, Rebecca, 139
Circular 230, 168
ClientWhys, 129
community colleges, 12–14, 25, 91
Covey, Stephen, 16
CPA Site Solutions, 129
Craigslist, 14, 100, 138

D

Damis, Beth, 147
Dreamweaver, 123
Dropbox, 127

E

eBay, 138
Edgar, Mark E., 76–78

Engagement Letter for Ongoing Client Services, 159–61
Engagement Letter for QuickBooks Setup, 156–58
Enrolled Agent designation (EA), 96, 155

F

Facebook, 30, 68, 131, 133, 175
finances
accounts receivable and collections, 148–49
billing rates and billing policies, 34, 100–101, 140–49
estimated tax payments, 60, 151
estimating income, 34–35
financial statements, 33, 34–35
full-time of part-time, 138–40
insurance, 150
organizations and memberships, 150
payments, 148–49
planning for expenditures, 150
retirement planning, 151
start-up costs, 14, 33–34, 137–38
tracking your time, 146, 147
forms
Articles of Formation, 59
Articles of Incorporation, 59, 61
Articles of Organization, 59, 64, 183–86
Election by a Small Business Corporation (Form 2553), 64
Form 1040-ES, 151
Form 1065, 61
Form 1120 and Form 1120-S, 61–64
from the Missouri Secretary of State's website, 182–89
Registration of Fictitious Name, 59, 60, 61, 187
Schedule C, 60, 64
Schedule K-1, 61
SS-4 Application for Employer ID Number (EIN), 64–65, 182, 188–89
SS-8 Determination of Worker Status for Purposes of Federal Employment Taxes and Income Tax Withholding, 27
1099s, 26–27, 65
Fundamental Payroll Certification (FPC), 96

G

Gier, Richard E., 62–63
GoDaddy, 122–23
Gomez, Nancy, 21

Google
    Blogger, 130
    Google Analytics, 124
    Google Places, 124
    Google Talk and Google Voice apps, 82
    registering your website, 124
    and sample forms, 182
    and social media sites, groups and forums,
        132, 135

H
home office. *See also* technology and the
        Internet
    accounting software, 83–86
    checklist, 88–89
    computer monitors, 80
    computers, 75–81
    and ergonomics, 73
    faxes, 82
    file cabinets, 74
    furniture and fixtures, 72–75
    lighting, 74
    miscellaneous items, 75
    office supplies, 87–90
    phones and headsets, 82
    printers and copiers, 80–81
    scanners, 81–82
    storage space and shelves, 75
    workspace, 70–72
HootSuite, 131
Hotmail, 174
HubSpot, 124
Hunter, Carolyn, 73

I
income taxes
    corporations, 61–64
    for employees and independent contractors,
        26–27
    estimated tax payments, 60, 151
    limited liability companies (LLC), 62, 64
    partnerships, 61, 62
    Schedule C, 60, 64
    sole proprietorships, 60, 62
InfoUSA, 105
insurance agents, 25, 31, 104, 150–51
Internal Revenue Service guidelines, 162–68
Intuit. *See* Quickbooks and Intuit

J
Joomla, 123

K
Kaniuk, Laura, 74
Kildal, Stacy, 149
Kilsheimer, Debra, 139

L
LeapFILE, 128
LegalZoom, 59, 182
Lincoln, Laura, 6
LinkedIn, 14, 30, 68, 131, 132–33, 135, 175

M
marketing
    brand identities, 30, 67, 98
    competition, competitive factors, and analysis,
        31–33
    finding your first clients, 99–101, 139
    logos, 30, 67–68, 98
    mailing and contact lists, 103–4, 105–7
    marketing resources, 170
    online marketing, 30, 114–36
    referrals, 30–31, 85, 100, 101, 104–10
    research and competitive analysis, 32
    social media, networking and resources, 30–31,
        100, 104, 105, 108, 130–36, 171
    speaking and presenting seminars, 109–13
    targeting a niche, 101–3
    writing blogs or articles, 129–30
Massachusetts Society of Certified Public
        Accountants, 162–68
Meyer, Martin G., 6
Miceli-Muhlbauer, Joan, 15, 71
Microsoft
    Microsoft Office, 79, 86
    Microsoft Office Live, 117–22
    Microsoft Publisher, 117, 123
MicroVision, 176
Mozy, 80
MSN, 124
MyCorporation, 59, 182

About the Author

Michelle L. Long, CPA, MBA is the owner of Long for Success, LLC (www.Long forsuccess.com) specializing in QuickBooks consulting and training services as well as coaching small business owners to start and grow their business. Michelle has a unique relationship with Intuit as an elite national trainer and presents "What's New for QuickBooks" to accounting professionals nationwide. She is a member of Intuit's Trainer/Writer Network and a consultant for Product development. She is an Advanced Certified ProAdvisor with other certifications as well. She is also the author of *Successful QuickBooks Consulting: The Comprehensive Guide to Starting and Growing a QuickBooks Consulting Business.*

Since 2000, Michelle has taught hundreds of QuickBooks seminars to thousands of QuickBooks users and accounting professionals. She has recorded QuickBooks courses that are sold as online training, DVDs, and even an iPad app. In addition to seminars, Michelle has conducted numerous webinars for Intuit and webcasts for Office Depot.

Michelle was named a Financial Services Champion of the Year for 2007 by the Small Business Administration in recognition of her dedication to helping entrepreneurs and small business owners. She is a Certified FastTrac Facilitator and has facilitated the Kauffman Foundation's FastTrac NewVenture program many times. She has been instrumental in helping hundreds of entrepreneurs and small business owners with their business or strategic plan.

Michelle has been mentioned in the *New York Times, Business Week, Investor's Business Daily, Accounting Today* and various blogs. She was named as one of "10 Worth Watching: Women who Inspire a Profession" by *Accounting Today.*

Michelle is the owner of the largest LinkedIn group (5,000+ members and growing) for accounting professionals, bookkeepers, Intuit employees, vendors and more. Feel free to join in the great discussions, news, and job postings too. The group is called Successful QuickBooks Consultants / Consulting.